THE PATH OF THE WORSHIPFUL SERVANTS

THE PATH OF
THE WORSHIPFUL
SERVANTS

To the Garden of the Lord of all the Worlds

Minhāj al-ʿĀbidīn ilā Jannati Rabbi 'l-ʿĀlamīn

by

Imām Ḥujjat al-Islām
ABŪ ḤĀMID AL-GHAZĀLĪ

Translated by
MUHTAR HOLLAND

AMAL PRESS
BRISTOL • ENGLAND

Amal Press, PO Box 688, Bristol BS99 3ZR, England

http://www.amalpress.com
info@amalpress.com

ISBN 978-0-9552359-8-6 paperback

Cover design: Abdallateef Whiteman/CDWM

Special thanks to Muhtar Holland for inspiring us all and Moutasem Atiya for making this publication possible. We also wish to thank Mian and Zakia Subhani and Ghalib Hussain for their invaluable donations.

CONTENTS

AUTHOR'S INTRODUCTION

IT WAS THE righteous and ascetic jurist [faqīh], Shaikh ʿAbd al-Malik (may God grant him forgiveness) who said: "This concise book was dictated to me by my most splendid Shaikh, the ascetic, fortunate and successful Imām, the Proof of Islam [Ḥujjat al-Islam], the Adornment of the Religion [Zain ad-Dīn], the Honor of the Community [Sharaf al-Umma], Abū Ḥāmid Muḥammad ibn Muḥammad ibn Muḥammad al-Ghazālī aṭ-Ṭūsī (God sanctify his spirit and exalt his degree in the Garden of Paradise). It is the very last book that he composed, and none received it from him by way of dictation, except the special elite of his companions."

[Imām al-Ghazālī said]: Praise be to God, the Sovereign [al-Malik], the Wise [al-Ḥakīm], the Generous [al-Jawād], the Noble [al-Karīm], the Glorious [al-ʿAzīz], the All-Compassionate [ar-Raḥīm], the One who created the human being in the fairest stature,[1] and created the heavens and the earth with His Power, and arranged all matters in the two abodes [of this world and the Hereafter] with His Wisdom, and did not create the jinn and humankind except for His worshipful service.[2] The path toward Him is evident to the aspiring travelers, and the signpost to Him is clearly visible to those who look, but God ﷻ causes whom He wills to go astray, and guides aright whomever He wills, *and He knows best the rightly guided* (6:117). May His blessings be upon the

Chief of the Messengers [Sayyid al-Mursalīn], and on the righteous, good and pure members of his family, and may He grant them peace and honor until the Day of Judgment.

You must realise, O my brethren (may God favour you and me with His good pleasure), that worshipful service [ʿibāda] is the fruit of knowledge [ʿilm], the benefit of life [ʿumr], the income of strong servants, the stock-in-trade of the saints [awliyā'], the path of the truly devout, the allotted portion of the mighty, the goal of those endowed with aspiration, the emblem of the noble, the vocation of real men, and the choice of those with faculties of vision. It is the way of good fortune and the path [minhāj] of the Garden of Paradise. God ﷻ has told us: *And I am your Lord, so worship Me* (21:92). He has also said: *Behold, this is a reward for you. Your endeavour has found acceptance* (76:22).

We, therefore, looked into the subject of worshipful service, and made a careful study of its path, from its beginnings to its destinations, which are the desired goals of its travelers. It is indeed a rugged path and a hard road, fraught with many obstacles, serious hardships, remote distances, enormous difficulties, frequent hindrances and impediments. It is beset with deadly perils and interruptions, abounding in enemies and highway robbers, and offering very few companions and followers. This is exactly how it needs to be, since it is the path of the Garden of Paradise, and this represents a confirmation of the saying of the Prophet ﷺ: "The Garden of Paradise is indeed surrounded by things that are repugnant [makārih], while the Fire of Hell is surrounded by objects of lustful desire [shahawāt]." He also said: "The Garden of Paradise is indeed a rugged ground on a hill, while the Fire of Hell is indeed a smooth ground in a sequestered courtyard."

Then, in addition to all of that, the servant [of the Lord] is weak, the time is difficult, and religious commitment is subject to retrogression. There is little leisure and much preoccupation. Life is short, and there is incapacity in work. The critic is perceptive, and the appointed term is near. The journey is long, and worshipful obedience [ṭāʿa] is the necessary provision, but it is transitory, so there is no replacement for it. If someone succeeds in obtaining it, he has triumphed, and he will enjoy good fortune for the eternity of those who are eternal [abada 'l-ābidīn] and for the endless duration of those who are everlasting [*dahra 'd-dāhirīn*]. If someone misses that, however, he will suffer loss together with the losers, and perish together with those who perish.

This therefore becomes, by God, a highly problematic affair, and the danger involved is enormous. That is why those who set out on this path are very few and far between. Then rare are those travelers who reach the destination and obtain the object sought. Then rarest of all are those who are chosen by God ﷻ to receive His intimate knowledge [*maʿrifa*] and His love [*maḥabba*], and whom He guides with His enabling grace [*tawfīq*] and His protection [*ʿiṣma*], then causes them, by His gracious favour, to attain to His good pleasure [*riḍwān*] and His Garden of Paradise. So we ask Him (Glorious is His remembrance) to include all of you, and us, among those who are triumphantly successful through His mercy.

Yes, indeed. Once we had discovered this path, and found that it matched the above description, we focused our attention on the manner in which it could be traversed. We tried to determine what the servant [of the Lord] would need, in the way of preparation, equipment, instruments, and skills, in terms of both knowledge and practise, so that he might traverse the path in safety, with the benefit of God's enabling grace [*tawfīq*], and not be trapped in its perilous obstacles, so that he would perish along with those who are doomed to perdition. The only sure refuge is with God [*wa 'l-ʿiyādhu bi'llāh*]!

We therefore composed several books on the subject of traversing and traveling this path, such as *Iḥyā' ʿUlūm ad-Dīn* [*The Revival of the Religious Sciences*], *al-Qurba ila 'llāhi (Taʿāla)* [*The Approach to God* ﷻ], and others besides. These works dealt with subtle aspects of the sciences, too abstruse for the understanding of the common folk, who consequently found fault with them, and wallowed in what they did not comprehend about them. Ah well, what speech is more eloquent than the speech of the Lord of All the Worlds? Yet they dismissed it as: "Mere fables of the men of old [*asāṭīru 'l-awwalīn*]."[3]

Have you not heard the words of Zain al-ʿĀbidīn ʿAlī, the son of al-Ḥusain, the son of Alī, the son of Abū Ṭālib ﷺ? It was he who said:

I will surely conceal the jewels of my knowledge,
   lest the ignorant should see them and act misguidedly.
In this respect, the father of Ḥasan has preceded
   al-Ḥusain, and has given good advice before him.
Oh, many a jewel of knowledge, if I should disclose it,

> I would be told: "You are one of those who worship idols!"
> Muslim men would consider it lawful to shed my blood,
> regarding the ugliest deed they commit as something good.

In the opinion of those devoted to religion [*dīn*], they being the noblest of God's creatures, the matter called for sympathetic consideration of all the creatures of God 🕮, and for the abandonment of contentious dispute. I therefore made humble supplication to the One who holds in His hand the creation and the commandment, beseeching Him to make it possible for me to compose a book—one that would meet with unanimous approval, and the reading of which would result in positive benefit.

That request of mine was granted by the One who responds to the distressed when he calls unto Him.[4] He made me privy, by His gracious favour, to the mysteries involved, and He inspired me with a marvellous arrangement, the like of which I did not recall in any of the previous compositions dealing with the secrets of religious practises. This is the arrangement I am applying to the present work, so I must say: "Enabling grace comes only through God [*bi'llāhi 't-tawfīq*]!"

When the servant [of the Lord] is first awakened to worshipful service [*'ibāda*], and devotes himself exclusively to traveling its path, he is motivated by a heavenly vibration from God 🕮, and a special enabling grace of Divine origin [*tawfīq khāṣṣ Ilāhī*]. This is what is signified by His words: *Is he whose breast God has expanded to receive Islam, so that he is guided by a light from his Lord [like one seized by ignorance]? (39:22).*

It has also been indicated by the [Prophet 🕮], the Master of the Sacred Law [*Ṣāḥib ash-Shar'*], for he said: "When the light enters the inner feeling, it expands and opens up." This prompted someone to ask: "O Messenger of God, is there any obvious sign by which that can be recognised?" He replied: "The shunning of the abode of illusion, turning in repentance to the abode of eternity, and being prepared for death before the advent of death."

THE HURDLE OF FOUR HINDRANCES

O SEEKER OF worshipful service, may God enable you to succeed! Your next obligation is to stop the hindrances [ʿawāriḍ] that distract you from the worshipful service of God ﷻ, and to block their access to you, so that they do not divert you from your goal. As we have mentioned earlier, they are four in number.

§ THE FIRST HINDRANCE: SUSTENANCE

The first hindrance is sustenance [rizq] and the demand of the lower self for its provision. Absolute trust [tawakkul] in God ﷻ is the only protection from this hindrance. You must therefore put all your trust in God ﷻ, in the matter of sustenance and in every case of need. That is for two reasons:

[First] freedom to engage in worship, and to receive the benefit of truly good provision. If someone is not absolutely trusting [mutawakkil], he is bound to be distracted from the worship of God ﷻ, because of the need for livelihood and welfare, either outwardly or inwardly. He is distracted either by the physical effort to acquire and to earn, like the common folk who are addicted to this world, or by desire and temptation [*waswasa*] experienced in the heart, like those who endeavour to worship but are still attached to this world.

Worshipful service needs freedom of the heart and the body, if it is to obtain its rightful due. Such freedom is peculiar to those who are absolutely trusting. I will even say, of everyone who is weak at heart, that his heart will scarcely be at ease without something known for sure, so it will hardly be satisfied with anything else, however great its importance in this world and the Hereafter. My Shaikh, Abū Muḥammad (may God bestow His mercy upon him), would often say in my hearing: "The business of this world goes well for two men: one who is absolutely trusting [*mutawakkil*], and one who is daring [*mutahawwir*]."

In my opinion, this statement is comprehensive in its meaning, since a person who is daring tackles affairs on the strength of habit and courage of heart, paying no attention to any obstacle that might prevent him, or any notion [*khāṭir*] that might weaken him, so things go well for him. As for someone who is absolutely trusting, he tackles affairs on the strength of conviction, discernment, perfect certitude concerning the promise of God ﷻ, and complete reliance on His guaranty. He pays no attention to anyone who tries to scare him, or to any devil who tries to tempt him, so he achieves his goals and succeeds in his endeavour.

As for the feeble creature, he is always caught between absolute trust, on the one hand, and hesitation, slackness, and confusion, on the other. He is like a donkey in its manger and a hen in its cage, noticing what its owner usually provides, and seldom bothering to look for anything else. His lower self takes no interest in lofty matters, and his aspiration is cut off, so he is unlikely to embark on any noble project. Even if he does so, he is unlikely to succeed in its accomplishment.

As you have surely noticed, the ambitious sons of this world have not achieved any major degree or important rank, except through their hearts' detachment from their lower selves, their properties and their families.

As for the kings, they engage in wars and in doing battle with their enemies, to the point of destruction or triumph, in order to obtain the rank of sovereignty and the authority of government. When Muʿāwiya ibn Sufyān saw the armies on the day of [the battle of] Ṣiffin, he said: "If someone wishes for something of great worth, he must run the great risk involved."

As for the traveling merchants, they ride dangers and perils by land and by sea, and they cast their persons and their properties into risky places in the east and in the west. They concentrate on one of two matters: either the deliverance of their spirits [*arwāḥ*], or the acquisition of profits [*arbāḥ*], in order to obtain every mighty profit, every massive property, and every precious object.

As for the market tradesman, whose heart is feeble and whose resolve is flimsy, he is unlikely to sever his heart from its attachment to his lower self and his property. He spends all his life between his home and his shop, so he never achieves a noble rank, like the kings, nor an enormous profit, like the merchants who dare to take risks. If, in his market, he makes the profit of a dirham [silver coin] on his goods, that is a great deal for him, because of his heart's attachment to something known for sure.

Up to this point, we have been discussing this world and its sons. As for the sons of the Hereafter, their capital investment is this virtue of absolute trust [in God] and severance of the heart from all attachments. Once they have consolidated this virtue and achieved it really and truly, they become free to worship God ﷻ. They become capable of isolation from fellow creatures, of traveling in the land, of penetrating the deserts, and of dwelling on the mountains and in the canyons. They have become the strong servants, the heroes of the religion, the freemen of humanity and the kings of the earth. They really do travel wherever they wish, and settle wherever they wish. They embark on tremendous undertakings, with knowledge and in worshipful service, as they see fit. They encounter no impediment, and no barrier stands in their way. All places for them are one, and all times are one in their view. This is indicated by the saying of the Prophet ﷺ:

> If someone takes pleasure in being the strongest of human beings, let him put all his trust in God ﷻ. If someone takes pleasure in being the noblest of human beings, let him practise true devotion to God ﷻ. If someone takes pleasure in being the richest of human beings, let him be more reliant on what is at God's disposal than on what is at his own disposal.

According to Sulaimān al-Khawwāṣ: "If a man puts all his trust in God ﷻ, with truthful intention, he has no need of the worldly commanders and those beneath them. How could he need them, when his Master is the Independent, the Praiseworthy?"

According to Ibrāhīm al-Khawwāṣ: "I met a young man in the wilderness, and he seemed like an ingot of silver, so I said to him: 'Where are you going, O young man?' He said: 'To Mecca.' I said: 'Without provision for the journey, and without a camel?' He said: 'O weak in certitude, He who can preserve the heavens and the earth is capable of bringing me to Mecca, without provision for the journey and without a camel!' When I entered Mecca, there he was, performing the *ṭawāf* [circumambulation of the Kaʿba] and saying:

> O self of mine, keep traveling forever,
>> and do not fall in love with anyone,
> except the Majestic Lord, the Everlasting.
> O self of mine, die of heartsickness.

"When he saw me, he said: 'O Shaikh, you're still in the state of weakness!'" Abū Muṭīʿ said to Ḥātim al-Aṣamm: "I have heard that you traverse the deserts with absolute trust [in God], without any provision for the journey." Ḥātim replied: "My provision for the journey consists of four things." Abū Muṭīʿ asked: "What are they?" He said: "I regard this world and the Hereafter as a dominion belonging to God ﷻ. I regard all creatures as the servants of God ﷻ and His dependants. I see the means of sustenance, and all other means, at the disposal of God ﷻ. I see that God's decree is effective in all of God's earth." The poet expressed it well, when he said:

> I see the abstainers enjoying fragrance and comfort.
>> Their hearts are far removed from this world.
> When you look at them, you are looking at people
>> who are kings of the earth, their mark being tolerance.

As for the second factor that necessitates absolute trust in God ﷻ in this matter [of sustenance], it is the tremendous danger and risk involved in the omission of that trust. God ﷻ has surely linked the provision of sustenance to the act of creation, for He has said: *God is the One who created you, then provided for you* (30:40).

This indicates that sustenance comes from God ﷻ, not from any other source, such as creatures. He did not confine Himself to the indication, however, for He added the promise: *God is indeed the All-Provider* (51:58). Nor did He confine Himself to the promise, for He added the guaranty: *There is no beast upon the earth for which God does not provide* (11:6). Nor did confine Himself to the guaranty, for He went on to swear: *And by the Lord of the heavens and the earth, it is the truth, even as that you speak* (51:23). Then, in addition to all that, He commanded absolute trust, and emphasised it with the admonition: *And put all your trust in the Living One who never dies* (25:58). He also said: *And put all your trust in God, if you are true believers* (5:23).

If someone fails to consider His saying, and is not content with His promise, and is not satisfied with His guaranty, and is not convinced by His oath, and then ignores His commandment, His promise and His threat, imagine what his state will be! What tribulation will result from this? This, by God, is a serious affliction, and we are guilty of great heedlessness if we ignore it. The truthful and trustworthy Messenger 🙵 once said to Ibn ʿUmar: How will it be for you, if you are left among a set of people who hoard their annual supply of sustenance, because of the weakness of their certitude?

We are told that al-Ḥasan [al-Baṣrī] (may God bestow His mercy upon him) once said: "May God curse any groups of people to whom their Lord swears an oath, yet they do not believe Him. When this Qurʾānic verse was revealed: *And by the Lord of the heavens and the earth....* (51:23)—the angels said: 'Perish the sons of Adam [human beings]! They angered the Lord until He swore that He would provide their sustenance.'"

According to Uwais al-Qaranī 🙵: "Even if you worship God with the worshipful service of the people of the heavens and the earth, He will not accept it from you, until you acknowledge that He speaks the truth." Someone asked: "And how shall we acknowledge that He speaks the truth?" Uwais replied: "You must be convinced of what God has destined for you, in the matter of your sustenance, and set your body free to worship Him." Harim ibn Ḥayyān said to him: "Where do you command me to reside?" Uwais pointed his hand towards Damascus, then Harim asked: "What is the cost of living there?" Uwais said: "Ugh! Alas for these hearts! Suspicion has infected them, so they derive no benefit from good advice."

We have heard that a body-snatcher [*nabbāsh*] repented at the hand of Abū Yazīd al-Bisṭāmī 🙵, so Abū Yazīd asked him about his condition, and he said: "I snatched bodies from a thousand graves, and I did not see their faces turned towards the *qibla* [direction of prayer], except the faces of two men." Abū Yazīd exclaimed: "Wretched are all those others, for doubt concerning sustenance turned their faces away from the *qibla*!"

One of our companions (may God bestow His mercy upon him) told me that he saw a man who was one of the people of righteousness, so he asked him about his spiritual state, saying: "Are you secure in your faith?" The man replied: "Faith is only secure for those who are absolutely trusting [in God]." We beg God 🕮 to improve us by His gracious favour, and not to chastise us for our mistakes. He is indeed the Most Merciful of the merciful.

You may say: "Tell us what is the real meaning of absolute trust, what is its legal status, and to what extent is it incumbent on the servant in the matter of sustenance?"

This will be explained to you in four subsections, concerning: (1) the linguistic derivation of the term *tawakkul* [absolute trust]; (2) its use in context; (3) its definition; and (4) its stronghold or fortress.

As for its linguistic derivation, *tawakkul* is a verbal noun formed on the pattern *tafaʿʿul*, derived from the same root, w–k–l, as *wakāla* [trusteeship; agency]. If a person is *mutawakkil* [trusting] in someone, he is appointing him as the *wakīl* [trustee; agent] in charge of his business, as the guarantor of its good management and as its caretaker, without imposing inconvenience and anxiety.

As for its use in context, you should know that *tawakkul* is an appropriate term in three contexts: (1) In the context of destiny [*qisma*], where it signifies confidence in God 🕮, because you will not lose what has been destined for you, since His judgement does not change, and this is established by hearing [the Qur'ān]. (2) In the context of help, where it signifies belief and confidence in the help you will receive from God 🕮, if you help Him and strive in His cause. God 🕮 has said: *And when you are firmly resolved, put all your trust in God* (3:159); and *He said: O you who truly believe, if you help God, He will help you* (47:7); and *It is incumbent on Us to help the true believers* (30:47). This is established by the promise He has given. (3) In the context of sustenance and need, for God 🕮 is responsible for whatever will make your physical constitution fit for His service, and whatever will enable you to worship Him. We know that from His saying: *And if someone puts all his trust in God, He will suffice him* (65:3). The truthful and trustworthy Messenger 🕮 once said: "If you put your trust in God 🕮, with the trust He fully deserves, He will sustain you as He sustains the birds, which leave their nests hungry in the morning, and return in the evening with their bellies full."

This is a binding duty for the servant, as indicated by the intellect and the Sacred Law together. This is the most obvious and compelling conclusion with regard to absolute trust [*tawakkul*] in the context of sustenance, and it is the purpose of this subsection.

Sustenance is guaranteed, according to those who are well versed in the knowledge of God ﷻ, but this will only be made clear to you by explaining the several categories of sustenance. You must therefore know that sustenance is subdivided into four categories: (1) that which is guaranteed; (2) that which is destined; (3) that which is already possessed, and (4) that which is promised [by God].

As for the sustenance that is guaranteed [*ma'mūn*], it is the nourishment by which the physical constitution is sustained without other means. The guaranty from God ﷻ applies to this kind of sustenance, and absolute trust is necessary in relation to it, as indicated by the intellect and the Sacred Law. Since God ﷻ has charged us with service and obedience to Him, with our bodies, He has guaranteed whatever will prevent deficiency in the physical constitution, so that we may perform what He has imposed upon us.

One of the shaikhs of the Karrāmiyya sect expressed himself fluently, on the basis of his heretical doctrine, when he said: "The guaranty of the servants' means of sustenance is necessary, in accordance with the wisdom of God ﷻ, for three reasons: (1) He is the Master and we are the servants, and it is incumbent on a master to provide for his servants, just as the servants must work for their master. (2) He has created them in need of sustenance, and He has not given them any means to obtain it, since they do not know what constitutes their sustenance, where it is, and when it is available. It is therefore incumbent on Him to supply that need of theirs, and to enable them to obtain their sustenance. (3) He has made them responsible for service, and the search for sustenance is a distraction from that. It is therefore incumbent on Him to supply them with sufficient provision, so that they can devote themselves to service."

This is the saying of someone who has not grasped the secrets of Lordship [*Rubūbiyya*]. If someone maintains that the provision of sustenance is incumbent on God ﷻ, he is in error, as we have explained in the discussion of [orthodox Islamic] theology [*fann al-kalām*].

Let us now return to our explanation of the four types of sustenance:

As for the sustenance that is destined [*maqsūm*], it is that which God ﷻ has foreordained and inscribed on the Well-kept Tablet [*al-Lawḥ al-Maḥfūẓ*]. It consists of what each individual will eat, drink, and wear, in a predetermined quantity and at a particular time. It will neither increase nor diminish, and neither be brought forward nor delayed, from what has been inscribed as its destiny. As the Prophet ﷺ once said: "Sustenance is unalterably foreordained. The righteousness of a righteous person cannot increase it, not can the profligacy of a profligate diminish it."

As for the sustenance that is already possessed [*mamlūk*], it is the worldly property owned by every individual, inasmuch as God ﷻ has decreed and foreordained that he should possess it, for it is part of the sustenance of God ﷻ. He has said: *Spend from that with which We have provided you* (2:254). In other words: "[Spend] from that which We have put in your possession."

As for the sustenance that is promised [*mawʿūd*], it is that which God ﷻ has promised to His truly devoted servants, on the condition of true devotion, as lawful sustenance obtained without trouble and toil. God ﷻ has said: *And if someone is truly devoted to God, He will prepare a way out for him, and He will provide for him from sources he could never imagine* (65:2–3). We have now described the four types of sustenance. Absolute trust is obligatory only in relation to the type that is guaranteed [*maʾmūn*], so understand that well!

As for the definition of absolute trust [*tawakkul*], according to one of our shaikhs: "It is the heart's reliance [*ittikāl*] on God ﷻ, with exclusive dependence on Him and despair of everything other than Him."

One of them said: "[It is] total commitment of the heart to God ﷻ, in relation to welfare, by abandoning its attachment to anything other than Him." According to Shaikh al-Imām Abū ʿUmar (may God bestow His mercy upon him): "Absolute trust [*tawakkul*] is the abandonment of attachment [*taʿalluq*], and attachment means attributing the maintenance of your physical constitution to something other than God ﷻ."

According to my own Shaikh, [Imām Abū Bakr al-Warrāq] (may God bestow His mercy upon him): "Absolute trust and attachment are two attributions. Absolute trust means attributing the maintenance of your physical constitution to God ﷻ, while attachment means attributing its maintenance to someone other than God ﷻ."

In my opinion, these sayings all refer to one basic principle: namely, that you must make your heart firmly convinced that the maintenance of your physical constitution, the satisfaction of your need, and your sufficient provision, all come directly from God 🕮, not by way of someone other than God, not by way of any ephemeral things of this world, and not by any secondary means whatsoever. Then, if God 🕮 so wills, He may put some created material or worldly means at His servant's disposal, or, if He so wills, He may suffice him directly with His power, without secondary means and indirect methods. If you remember that with your heart, and are firmly convinced that it is true, and if the heart is completely devoted to God 🕮 and to Him alone, to the exclusion of created objects and secondary means, you will then have attained to the reality of absolute trust. Such is its definition.

As for the stronghold of absolute trust, which supports its attainment, it is the remembrance of God's guaranty. The stronghold of its stronghold is the remembrance of God's majesty and His perfection, in His knowledge, His sustenance, His power, and His total freedom from breaking promises, absent-mindedness, inadequacy, and deficiency. If the servant is diligent in remembering all these points, he will attain to absolute trust in God 🕮 where the matter of sustenance is concerned.

You may ask: "Is there any situation whatsoever, in which the servant is obliged to search for sustenance?"

You must therefore know that guaranteed sustenance is that which provides nourishment and support [for the physical constitution]. We cannot search for it, since it is part of what God 🕮 does for His servant. Like life and death, the servant can neither procure it nor drive it away. As for that which is allotted by indirect means, the servant is not obliged to search for it, since he has no need for that search. His only need is for that which is guaranteed, and that comes directly from God 🕮 and within the guaranty of God 🕮.

As for His saying, *And seek the gracious favour of God* (62:10)—it refers to [the search for] knowledge and spiritual reward, though some say: "No, it is a special concession, since it is a commandment in the wake of the prohibition,[5] so it is meant in the sense of permission, not in the sense of necessity and obligation."

Someone may say: "But this guaranteed sustenance is provided by indirect means. Is it necessary for us to seek those means?"

The answer will be: That is not required of you, since the servant has no need of it. God 🕮 does His work by indirect means and without indirect means, so why should you need to seek the indirect means? Besides, God 🕮 has given you an absolute guaranty, without the condition of seeking and earning. God 🕮 has said: *There is no beast upon the earth for which God does not provide its sustenance* (11:6).

That being the case, how can it befit Him to command the servant to search for something, when he does not know where to look for it? Of all the available means, he has no idea which will give him access to his sustenance, not to something else. He cannot tell which will be his means of nourishment and growth, not something else. Not one of us can identify the particular means required for that purpose, so it would not make sense to impose that search upon him. Consider this correctly, for it is very clear.

Besides, it should be enough for you to know that the prophets 🕮 and the saints who put all their trust in God 🕮 did not seek any sustenance—in most cases and in general—and they devoted themselves exclusively to worshipful service. The consensus is that they would never fail to comply with God's commandment, and they would never disobey Him in that respect. It must therefore be clear to you that searching for sustenance and its means of obtainment is not a necessary undertaking for the servant.

You may ask: "Is sustenance increased by searching, and is it reduced by the failure to search?"

My answer will be: Certainly not, for it is inscribed on the Well-kept Tablet, foreordained and fixed in time. There is no changing of God's decree, and no altering of His destiny and His inscription. This is correct according to our scholars, contrary to the opinion held by some of the companions of Ḥātim [al-Aṣamm] and Shaqīq [al-Balkhī], who said: "Sustenance is not increased or diminished by the action of the servant, but property [*māl*] does increase and diminish." This is incorrect, because the evidence in both cases is one and the same, that being the inscription [on the Well-kept Tablet] and destiny [*qisma*], and it is indicated by His saying: *So that you do not grieve for what has escaped you, nor exult because of what you have been given* (57:23).

If it was indeed increased by searching and reduced by the failure to search, it would be a cause of grief or exultation, since the servant would be slack and lazy until it escaped him, or vigorous and energetic until he acquired it. The Prophet ﷺ said to a beggar [who asked him for a dry date]: "Here you are! If you do not come and get it, it will surely come to you!"

It may be said: "The reward and the punishment are also inscribed on the Well-kept Tablet, and we are obliged to seek the reward and refrain from the cause of punishment, so are reward and punishment increased by seeking or reduced by refraining?"

You must therefore know that seeking the reward is necessary only because God has commanded it with a definite commandment, and threatened punishment for its omission. He has not guaranteed the reward without any action on our part, and increasing the reward and the punishment depends on the action of the servant. The difference between the two is a subtle point, for according to one of our scholars: "The inscription on the Well-kept Tablet is in two parts:

The FIRST PART is inscribed absolutely and unconditionally, with no dependence on the action of the servant. This is the list of the provisions of sustenance [*arzāq*] and the appointed terms of life [*ājāl*]. Notice how God ﷻ has mentioned both of them absolutely and without condition. He has said: *There is no beast upon the earth for which God does not provide its sustenance* (11:6). And He has said: *When their term comes, they shall neither tarry for a moment nor forge ahead* (7:34).

The Master of the Sacred Law [the Prophet ﷺ] once said: Four things have been finally determined: (1) the creation [*khalq*]; (2) nature [*khuluq*]; (3) sustenance [*rizq*]; and (4) the appointed term [*ajal*].

The SECOND PART is inscribed with a condition, making it dependent on the action of the servant. This is the list of the reward and the punishment [to be meted out at the Resurrection]. Notice how God ﷻ has mentioned them both in His Book [the Qur'ān], where He makes them dependent on the action of the servant. He has said: *If only the People of the Book would believe and practise true devotion, We would remit their sins from them and We would bring them into Gardens of Delight* (5:65).

This is very clear, so understand it well!

Someone may say: "In our experience, the seekers find provisions and properties, while the abstainers are deprived and impoverished!"

He will be told: From what you say, it seems that you do not find a seeker deprived and poor, or an abstainer at leisure, prosperous, and rich. Yes indeed, this is the most common state of affairs! You should know that this is the foreordainment of the Almighty, the All-Knowing, and the management of the Sovereign, the All-Wise.

Abū Bakr Muḥammad ibn Sābiq, the preacher from Ṣaqalliyya in Syria (may God bestow His mercy upon him), recited these poetic verses:

> From many a strong man, strong in his versatility
>   and mentally acute, sustenance veers away,
> while many a weakling, weak in his versatility,
>   seems to be scooping plenty from the ocean gulf.
> This is a sign that God has secret knowledge
>   of His creatures, a secret that is not disclosed.

You may ask: "Should you enter the desert without provision for the journey?" The answer is that, if you have strength of heart in relation to God ﷻ, and complete reliance on God's promise, you should enter [without provision]; if not, stay with the common folk and their attachments. I heard Imām Abu'l-Maʿālī (may God bestow His mercy upon him) say: "If someone stays close to God ﷻ, while following the custom of the common folk, God will stay close to him in supplying sufficient provision." This is a very fine saying, containing abundant benefits for those who consider it with care.

You may ask: Does not God ﷻ say: *So make provision for yourselves, for the best provision is true devotion* (2:197). You must therefore know that this contains two statements: (1) That it [the provision you must make for yourselves] is the provision for the Hereafter. That is why He said: "The best provision is true devotion," and He did not say: "the vanities of this world and its material means." (2) That some people did not take provision for themselves on the journey to the Pilgrimage, relying on other people instead. They would beg and complain, pestering and annoying other people, so they were commanded to make provision for themselves, with an admonition to the effect that taking provision from your own property is better than taking other people's property and relying on them.

You may also ask: "Does this mean that, if someone is absolutely trusting [in God], he should still carry provision with him on journeys?"

You must therefore know that he may carry provision, but he should not attach his heart to it, with the conviction that it is undoubtedly his sustenance, and that it contains his physical support. He should attach his heart solely to God ﷻ, put all his trust in Him, and say: "Sustenance is allotted by destiny, unalterably predetermined. If God ﷻ so wills, He will support my physical constitution with this or with something else." He may also carry provision with some other intention, to assist a fellow Muslim, for instance.

The essence of the matter is not about taking provision or traveling without it, but rather about the heart. You must not attach your heart to anything but the promise of God ﷻ, the excellence of His sufficiency, and His guaranty. Many a traveler carries provision, though his heart is with God, not with the provision. Many a traveler leaves provision behind, though his heart is with the provision, not with God ﷻ. What really matters, therefore, is the heart. You must understand these principles, for then you will have enough to meet your needs, if God ﷻ so wills.

Someone may say: "The Prophet ﷺ used to carry provision for the journey, as did the Companions ﷺ and the righteous predecessors."

He will be told: That is unquestionably permissible [*mubāḥ*], not unlawful [*ḥarām*]. The only thing that is unlawful is attaching the heart to the provision, and forsaking absolute trust in God ﷻ, so understand that well! Besides, what do you think of God's Messenger ﷺ, considering that God ﷻ told him: *And put all your trust in the Living One who never dies* (25:58).

Did he disobey Him in that? Did he attach his heart to food and drink, or to a dirham [silver coin] or a dinar [gold coin]? Of course not, and God forbid that it should be so! No indeed, his heart was with God ﷻ, and his absolute trust was in God ﷻ, as He had commanded him, for he is the one who paid no attention whatsoever to this world, and never extended his hand to the keys of all the earth's treasures. When he ﷺ and the righteous predecessors took provision with them, they did so because of good intentions, not because their hearts were inclined towards the provision instead of towards God ﷻ. The important point is the intention, as we have informed you, so understand that well. Wake up from your slumber, arise from your heedlessness, and try to understand, for then God will guide you aright.

You may ask: "Which is more meritorious, taking provision for the journey, or leaving it behind?"

You must therefore know that this varies as the situation varies. If he is leading a caravan, the traveler may wish to demonstrate that taking provision is permissible, or he may intend to use it to assist a fellow Muslim, or to succour someone in distress. In cases such as these, taking provision is more meritorious. If he is traveling alone, and he is strong of heart in relation to God ﷻ, provision for the journey may distract him from the worshipful service of God ﷻ, so leaving it behind is more meritorious.

Try to understand all this, and practise it correctly. God is the Source of enabling grace!

§ THE SECOND HINDRANCE: PERILS AND DANGERS

The only protection from perils and dangers [akhṭār] resides in delegation [tafwīḍ]. You must therefore delegate the whole business to God ﷻ, and that is for two reasons.

1. The immediate calming of the heart. When situations are dangerous and dubious, so that you cannot distinguish what is right about them from what is wrong, you experience disturbance in your heart and confusion in your natural instincts. You cannot tell whether you are becoming involved in something virtuous, or in something corrupt. Then, when you delegate the whole business to God ﷻ, you know that you will not become involved in anything that is not virtuous and good. You will thus feel safe from danger, mischief and transgression, as your heart becomes tranquil at once. This tranquillity, security and comfort in the heart is a tremendous advantage. Our Shaikh (may God bestow His mercy upon him) would often say, during his meeting: "Leave the management to the One who created you, for then you may relax!" He also recited these poetic verses on the subject:

> When someone cannot tell whether his benefit
> resides in what is pleasing or what is unpleasant,
> it befits him to delegate what he cannot handle
> to the One who will look after all his needs,
> the Caring Diety [Ilāh], the One who is Kinder
> in compassion than his father and his mother.

2. The acquisition of what is right and good in the future. That is because conditions at the hurdles are ambiguous. Many an evil appears in the form of

something good, many a disadvantage assumes the guise of an advantage, and many a poison takes the shape of a honeycomb. You are ignorant of the hurdles and their mysteries. If you take matters at face value, and engage in them of your own volition, as you see fit, how quickly you will fall into perdition, while you are unaware!

It is related that one of the worshippers asked God ﷻ to let him see Iblīs, so he was told: "Ask for well-being!" He refused to accept anything other than that [the sight of Iblīs], so God ﷻ showed Iblīs to him. As soon as he saw Iblīs, the worshipper aimed a blow at him, so Iblīs said to him: "Were it not that you will live for a hundred years, I would surely destroy you and punish you!" The worshipper was deluded by these words, and he said to himself: "My life will be very long, so I shall do whatever I wish, then repent later on." He lapsed into depravity, abandoned worshipful service, and perished.

This should admonish you to refrain from making definite predictions, and from insisting on the fulfilment of your desire. It should also warn you against excessive expectation, for that is the great disaster. The poet spoke the truth when he said:

Beware of lustful desires and cravings,
    for many a craving has resulted in death.

If you delegate your business to God ﷻ, and ask Him to choose for you what is in your best interest, you will encounter only that which is good and correct. Quoting the words of a righteous servant [in Pharaoh's court], God ﷻ relates: *"And I delegate my business to God. God is Ever-Perceptive of the servants"* (40:44). Then He went on to say: *So God warded off from him the evils which they plotted, while a dreadful doom encompassed Pharaoh's folk* (40:45).

Notice how He made the servant's delegation [to Him] result in protection from evils, assistance against the enemies, and achievement of the goal. You must consider this successfully, if God ﷻ so wills.

You may say: "Explain to us the meaning of delegation [*tafwīḍ*] and its legal status."

You must therefore know that the term is best explained under two headings: (1) The context in which delegation [*tafwīḍ*] is appropriate, and its legal status. (2) Its meaning, its definition, and its opposite.

As for its proper context, know that objectives are three in number:

1. An objective about which you know for certain that it is wicked and evil, absolutely without doubt, like the Fire of Hell and the torment, and such actions as unbelief [*kufr*], heretical innovation [*bidʿa*] and sinful disobedience [*maʿṣiya*]. There can be no question of intending to achieve that objective.

2. An objective about which you know for certain that it is right and proper, like the Garden of Paradise, true belief, and the Sunna [exemplary practise of the Messenger 鑾], for instance. You are entitled to intend the attainment of such objectives, without reservation. Delegation is out of place in this context, since there is no danger involved, and no doubt that the objective is good and proper.

3. An objective about which you do not know for certain that it is right for you, or wrong: for instance, the performance of supererogatory devotions [*nawāfil*] and making use of things that are permissible [*mubāḥāt*]. This is the proper context of delegation. You are not allowed to intend such objectives without reservation, but only by making the intention contingent on the will of God [by saying: "If God wills [*in shāʾa 'llāh*]"] and conditional on goodness and correctness. If you restrict your intention by making it contingent on the will of God, that constitutes an act of delegation [*tafwīḍ*]. If you make your intention without saying: "If God wills [*in shāʾa 'llāh*]," that constitutes a blameworthy and forbidden desire.

Delegation is therefore appropriate in the context of every objective in which there is an element of danger, since you cannot be certain that it contains what is correct for you.

As for the meaning of delegation [*tafwīḍ*], according to one of our shaikhs (may God bestow His mercy upon them): "It is abstaining from the choice that involves some risk, and leaving it to the One who is qualified to choose and manage, the One who knows the best interest of His creatures. There is no god but He!" According to Shaikh Abū Muḥammad as-Sijzī (may God bestow His mercy upon him): "It is leaving your risky choice to the One who is qualified to choose [al-Mukhtār], so that He may choose what is best for you, on your behalf." According to Shaikh Abū ʿUmar (may God bestow His mercy upon him): "It is the abandonment of ambitious desire, and ambitious desire is the unconditional intention to achieve something risky." Such are the definitions offered by the shaikhs. Our own view is expressed as follows:

Delegation is the wish to have God ﷻ take care of your interests, in those cases where you do not feel safe from the danger involved. The opposite of delegation is ambitious desire [*tamaʿ*], but there are two aspects to the general concept of ambitious desire:

1. It signifies hope, in the sense that you wish for something that involves no danger, or for something risky, in which case you make your intention contingent on the will of God. That is praiseworthy, not blameworthy. As God ﷻ has said: *"And who, I ardently hope, will forgive me my sin on the Day of Doom"* (26:82); *"We ardently hope that our Lord will forgive us our sins, because we are the first of the believers"* (26:51). This aspect is not the one that concerns us here.

2. It signifies blameworthy ambition, as in the saying of the Prophet ﷺ: "Beware of ambitious desire, for it is a present poverty."

Someone said: "Ambitious desire is the destruction and corruption of the religion, and pious caution is its firm foundation." According to our Shaikh (may God bestow His mercy upon him): "Blameworthy ambition is twofold: (1) the heart's attachment to a suspicious benefit, and (2) the unconditional intention to achieve something risky."

As for the stronghold of delegation, it is remembering the danger inherent in situations, and the possibility of ruination and corruption they contain. The stronghold of its stronghold is remembering your inability to guard against the various kinds of peril, and to prevent yourself from falling into them, through your ignorance, your heedlessness and your weakness. Diligence in these two efforts of remembrance will induce you to delegate all matters to God ﷻ, to beware of predicting their achievement without reservation, and to refrain from intending them without making the intention contingent on goodness and correctness. God is the Source of enabling grace!

You may be asked: "What is this danger, because of which you consider delegation necessary in our affairs?"

You must therefore know that danger is a general term, covering two specific dangers:

1. The danger of doubt as to whether something will or will not be, and whether you will or will not achieve it. This requires *istithnāʾ* [making your intention contingent on the will of God], and it falls within the chapter of intention [*niyya*] and overexpectation [*amal*].

2. The danger of erroneous conduct, inasmuch as you are not certain that it contains what is right and proper for you. This is the situation in which delegation is necessary.

The leading scholars have provided differing explanations of danger. According to one of them: "The danger in taking an action is that there may be salvation in not taking it, for it may possibly involve a sin. There is no danger in true belief, right conduct and adherence to the Sunna, since salvation is absolutely impossible without true belief, and right conduct does not involve any sin. Where true belief and right conduct are concerned, it is therefore correct to intend their observance unconditionally."

According to the Professor [Abū Ishāq al-Isfarānī] (may God bestow His mercy upon him): "The danger in taking an action is that the danger may possibly present a hindrance, so that dealing with the hindrance becomes the main concern, rather than proceeding with the action. That may happen in connection with permissible actions [mubāḥāt], customary practises [sunan] and obligatory observances [farā'id]. Consider the case of someone who has barely enough time for the ritual prayer, so he intends to perform it, but he is suddenly threatened by a fire or a flood, from which it is possible for him to escape. In that situation, preoccupation with his escape is more appropriate than embarking on his ritual prayer. Unconditional intention is not correct, therefore, with regard to permissible and supererogatory practises and many obligatory observances."

Someone may ask: "How can it be fitting for God to impose something on His servant, and threaten him with punishment for its omission, if there is no benefit for him in its performance?"

You should therefore know that our Shaikh (may God bestow His mercy upon him) has said: "God ﷻ does not command the servant to do something, unless it is to his benefit and he is free from hindrances. He does not bind His servant to the performance of an obligatory duty, so strictly that he has no exemption from it, unless there is also benefit for him in that. God ﷻ may sometimes grant him an excuse, on the grounds that attending to one of two commandments is better than preoccupation with the other, as we have mentioned above. In that case, the servant is not only excused, but rewarded, not for omitting one obligatory duty, but for performing the other, which is more important."

I heard the Imām [Abu'l-Maʿālī] (may God bestow His mercy upon him) say this about this question: "In everything that God has imposed on His servants, such as the ritual prayer, the fast, and the pilgrimage, there is undoubtedly some benefit for the servant, and it is correct to intend their performance unconditionally." He added: "Our opinion on this is generally agreed." This means that permissible and supererogatory observances are subject to this rule [of delegation], so understand that well, for it is one of the abstruse topics of the chapter. God is the Source of enabling grace!

Someone may ask: "Is the delegator [*mufawwiḍ*] safe from perdition and maltreatment, when the abode [of this world] is the abode of trial and tribulation?"

You must therefore know that, in most cases, the delegator is only treated well. His treatment is rarely anything but good. If he does happen to be treated badly, he may be disappointed and so fall from the rank of delegation, though there is no benefit for the servant in disappointment and falling from the rank of delegation. This is the opinion of Shaikh Abū ʿUmar (may God bestow His mercy upon him).

It has also been said: "The delegator is treated only with what is to his benefit, in relation to what he has delegated to God ﷻ. As for disappointment and falling short of the rank of delegation, they are out of the question in this context, since there is no doubt as to their wrongness. Delegation applies only to something about which there is uncertainty concerning its wrongness and its rightness." This is the better of the two opinions, according to our own Shaikh (may God bestow His mercy upon him), since the incentive to delegation would otherwise not be strong.

It may be asked: "Is it obligatory for the delegator to receive the most excellent treatment?"

You must therefore know that obligation is absurd in reference to God ﷻ, for He is under no obligation to His servants. He may treat the servant with what is most beneficial, rather than what is most excellent, as an act of wisdom on His part. Consider how He decreed that the Prophet ﷺ and his Companions should sleep throughout the night until the rising of the sun, on one of their journeys, so that they missed the ritual prayer of the night and the ritual prayer of the dawn, even though prayer is more excellent than sleep. He would sometimes ordain that he should be preoccupied with wives and children, even though exclusive devotion to the worship of God ﷻ is more excellent, for, *He is Ever-Aware of His servants, All-Seeing* (42:27).

This is as the case of the skilled and wise physician, who chooses barley water for the invalid, even though sugar water is more excellent and sweeter, since he knows that barley water is more beneficial in treating his illness. The goal for the servant is salvation from perdition, not that which is [apparently] most excellent and most noble, though combined with corruption and destruction.

It may be asked: "Is the delegator free to choose?"

You must therefore know that the correct opinion, according to our scholars, is that he is free to choose, and is not subject to reproach concerning his delegation. That is because, if there is some benefit for him in surplus and what is more excellent, he will wish for God ﷻ to provide him with what is most excellent, just as the invalid will say to the physician: "Let my medicine be sugar water, instead of barley water, if there is some benefit for me in both, so that I may obtain the surplus and the benefit together." The case of the servant is similar, if he asks God ﷻ to include his benefit in what is most excellent, and to provide him therewith, so that He will grant him the surplus and the benefit together. This request must be made subject, however, to the condition that, if God chooses the benefit for him in some form other than the most excellent, he will be perfectly content with that.

It may be asked: "Why is the servant free to choose what is most excellent, though he is not free to choose what is most beneficial?"

You must understand that this is the difference between the two: The servant can distinguish the most excellent from the inferior, but he cannot distinguish the beneficial from the harmful, in order to seek it with unconditional intention. Besides, the meaning of his choosing the most excellent is that he wishes that God ﷻ provide him with his benefit included in what is most excellent, and for Him to choose and ordain that on his behalf. It does not mean that the servant has any control over anything in that regard, so understand that well!

There you have the gist of the subtle knowledge of this subject [of delegation] and its mysteries. Had the need for it not been so pressing, we would not have ventured on its exposition, because it is like the clashing waves of the oceans of the sciences of revelatory disclosure [*mukāshafa*]. In this book, I have confined myself to providing the essential information, with the intention of explaining it for the benefit of both the master scholars and the novices, if God ﷻ so wills. God is the Source of enabling grace!

§ THE THIRD HINDRANCE: DESTINY'S DECREE

The only protection from destiny's decree [*qaḍā'*] is contentment [*riḍā*] therewith. You must be content with God's decree ﷻ for two reasons:

1. Freedom to worship. That is because, if you are not content with destiny's decree, you will always be worried, for your heart will keep wondering: "Why was it like that, and why is it like this?" If your heart is preoccupied with these concerns, how can it be free to worship? You have only one heart and you have filled it with anxieties, with questions about the past and future state of this world, so what space is left in it for the remembrance of God, for His worship, and for thinking about the Hereafter?

Shaqīq [al-Balkhī] (may God bestow His mercy upon him) spoke the truth when he said: "By regretting things past and trying to manage those yet to come, you have lost the blessing of your present moment."

2. The danger of incurring the wrath of God ﷻ through discontent. As we learn from traditional reports, one of the prophets complained to God ﷻ about something unpleasant that had happened to him, so God ﷻ addressed him by way of inspiration, saying: "Do you lodge a complaint against Me, when I am not deserving of blame and complaint? This is how your situation appeared in the knowledge of the Unseen, so why are you displeased with My decree for you? Do you wish Me to alter this world for your sake, or to change the Well-kept Tablet [al-Lawḥ al-Maḥfūz] because of you, and so decree what you wish, instead of what I wish, and that it should be as you find pleasing, not as I find pleasing? By My Might and Glory, I swear that if you repeat this within your breast another time, I shall divest you of the garb of Prophethood and transport you to the Fire of Hell, and I shall not care!"

Let the intelligent person listen to this awesome admonition and the terrifying threat. If God can be like this with His prophets and His chosen friends, how will He be with others? Listen again to His saying ﷻ: "If you repeat this in your breast another time...." This relates to the prattle of the lower self and the vacillation of the heart, so how will it be for someone who screams and cries for help, who complains to his Lord, the Noble and Generous Benefactor, moaning and yelling over the heads of the congregation, and who attracts supporters and companions? This applies to someone who has been displeased on one occasion, so how will it be for someone who spends his whole life in displeasure with God ﷻ? This applies to someone who complains to Him, so how will it be for someone who complains to others?

We take refuge with God from the evils of our lower selves, and from the wickedness of our deeds. We beg Him to pardon us and forgive us for our misconduct, and to improve us with the excellence of His caring attention. He is indeed the Most Merciful of the merciful.

Someone may ask: "What is the meaning of contentment with destiny's decree? How can it be realised, and what is its legal status?"

You should therefore know that the scholars have said: "Contentment is the abandonment of displeasure. Displeasure is expressed by asserting that something other than what God ﷻ has decreed would be better and more beneficial for you, though you do not know for certain whether it is good or bad." This [abandonment of displeasure] is a precondition of contentment, so understand that well.

You may say: "Surely all evils and sins are due to the decree and foreordainment of God ﷻ, so how can the servant be content with evil, and how can that be incumbent upon him?"

You should therefore know that contentment with the decree is all that is incumbent. The decreeing of evil is not itself an evil. The evil is what has been decreed, so contentment is not with the evil [but only with the fact that God has decreed it]. According to our shaikhs ﷺ:

Four things have been divinely decreed: (1) a benefit [niʿma], (2) an adversity [shidda], (3) something good [khair], and (4) something evil [sharr].

In the case of a benefit, there must be contentment with the One who decrees [al-Qāḍī], the decree [al-qaḍāʾ], and what is decreed [al-maqḍī]. There must also be gratitude for it, inasmuch as it is a blessing, and the servant must acknowledge its blessedness by demonstrating the effect of the benefit.

In the case of an adversity, there must also be contentment with the One who decrees, the decree, and what is decreed. There must also be patience, since an adversity is hard to endure.

In the case of something good, there must also be contentment with the One who decrees, the decree, and what is decreed. The servant must also acknowledge the favour, since it is a boon that he has been fortunate to obtain.

In the case of something evil, there must also be contentment with the One who decrees, the decree, and what is decreed, inasmuch as it has been decreed, not inasmuch as it is evil. The fact that it has been decreed is attributable, in reality, to the decree and the One who decrees.

This last case is similar to the situation where you are content with the doctrine [*madhhab*] of the proponent of a different school, in the sense that you are content to have knowledge of it, not to adopt it as your own doctrine. The fact that it is known [*maʿlūm*] is attributable to knowledge [*ʿilm*], so you are actually content and pleased with the knowledge of that doctrine, not with the doctrine itself.

Someone may ask: "If someone is content, is he entitled to ask for more?" The answer will be: Yes, if he does so with the stipulation that it must be good and proper, not unconditionally. That will not dislodge him from contentment. It is actually a sign of contentment, so it is better [than not asking for more], because, if something delights a person and he is content with it, he will naturally ask for more of the same. The Prophet ﷺ used to say, when milk was available: "O God, grant us Your blessing in it, and provide us with more of it!" He would also say, when referring to [food or drink] other than milk: "[O God, grant us Your blessing in it], and provide us with more of something better than it!"

In neither case did he indicate that he was not content with what God ﷻ had foreordained for him in that particular instance.

You may ask: "Has it not been reported that the Prophet ﷺ made his request contingent on God's will, and conditional on its being good and proper?" You must therefore know that these matters are peculiar to the heart, and there is no need to express them with the tongue. Failure to express them verbally is therefore unimportant, provided they are stipulated by the heart, so understand that unequivocally.

§ THE FOURTH HINDRANCE: ADVERSITIES AND MISFORTUNES

There is only one protection from adversities [shadā'id] and misfortunes [maṣā'ib], and that is patience [ṣabr]. You must therefore practise patience in all situations. That is for two reasons:

1. The achievement of worshipful service and the accomplishment of its purpose. The whole business of worshipful service is founded on patience and the endurance of adversities, so, if someone is not patient, he will not achieve any part of it in reality. That is because, if someone intends to worship God ﷻ, and genuinely devotes himself to that worship, he will be confronted by adversities, trials, and misfortunes from several directions:

First of all, there is no worshipful service in which hardship is not an essential element. That accounts for all this encouragement to perform it, and the promise of reward. The performance of worship is impracticable without the curbing of passion and the subjugation of the lower self, since the lower self is an obstacle to all that is good. Resistance to passion and the subjugation of the lower self are among the most difficult challenges confronting the human being.

Secondly, if the servant does good work, in spite of the hardship involved, he is obliged to act with caution, so that his work will not be spoiled, and prudence is more exacting than the work itself.

Thirdly, the abode [of this world] is the abode of trial and tribulation, so its inhabitant will inevitably be afflicted with its adversities and misfortunes. There are several types of misfortune: misfortune afflicting the family, close relatives, spiritual brethren, and companions with death, loss, and separation; physical misfortune, in the form of diseases and ailments; misfortune affecting a person's reputation, so that people attack him, envy him, belittle him, and indulge in backbiting and telling lies about him; misfortune affecting property, by causing it to be lost and cease to exist. Each of these misfortunes inflicts a particular kind of ordeal and torment, so it is necessary to endure them all with patience. Anxiety and grief will otherwise deprive the servant of the freedom to worship.

Fourthly, the seeker of the Hereafter is always more severely afflicted and subject to more trial and tribulation. The closer someone is to God, the more he suffers misfortunes in this world, and the more severely he is tested. You have surely heard the saying of the Prophet ﷺ: "Of all human beings, those most severely tested are the prophets, then the scholars, then those who are most exemplary...."

If someone intends to do good work, and devotes himself completely to the path of the Hereafter, these trials and tribulations are therefore bound to confront him. If he does not endure them with patience, and fails to avoid preoccupation with them, he will be cut off from the path and distracted from worshipful service, so he will not achieve any part thereof. God ﷻ has told us to be on our guard against trials, tribulations and misfortunes, and the suffering they inflict upon us. He confirmed and emphasised that admonition, for He said: *Surely you will be tried in your property and in your persons, and you will hear much wrong from those who were given the Book before you, and from the idolaters* (3:186). Then He went on to say: *But if you endure with patience and practise true devotion, that represents the resolute handling of things* (3:186).

It is as if He were saying: "Convince yourselves firmly that you will inevitably suffer various kinds of trial and tribulation, then, if you endure with patience, you will be real men, and your resolutions will be the resolutions of real men." If someone is determined to worship God ﷻ, he must therefore resolve, first of all, to practise patience for a very long time, and to commit himself firmly to enduring the terrible adversities that will follow one another in succession until death. He will otherwise lose the means to achieve his goal, and approach it from the wrong direction.

We are told that al-Fuḍail (may God bestow His mercy upon him) once said: "If someone is determined to traverse the road to the Hereafter, let him install within himself these four colours of death: the white, the red, the black, and the green. The white death is hunger, the black is tolerance of blame from other people, the red is opposition to the devil, and the green is [indifference to] the succession of misfortunes, one after the other."

2. As for the second of the two reasons for patience, it is the benefit conferred by patience in this world and the Hereafter, including salvation and success. God ﷻ has said: *And if someone is truly devoted to God, He will prepare a way out for him, and He will provide for him from sources he could never imagine* (65:2–3).

In other words: "If someone is truly devoted to God ﷻ, with patience, He will grant him a way out of adversities, including victory over the enemies." God ﷻ has said: *So endure with patience, for the outcome is in favour of the truly de-*

vout (11:49). God ﷻ has also said: *And the fair word of the Lord was fulfilled for the Children of Israel, because of their patient endurance* (7:137).

Joseph ﷺ is said to have written, in response to Jacob ﷺ: "Your forefathers endured with patience, so they triumphed. You must therefore endure with patience, as they endured with patience, and triumph as they triumphed." In this same context, a poet has said:

> Do not despair, even if suffering is prolonged.
> If you seek help with patience, you will find relief.
> The patient sufferer well deserves to satisfy his need,
> and he who keeps knocking at the doors deserves refuge.

One of the benefits of patience is that it confers precedence and leadership. God ﷻ has said: *And We appointed them to be leaders guiding by Our command* (21:73). Those benefits include commendation from God ﷻ, for He has said: *We found him patiently enduring. An excellent servant indeed [was the Prophet Job], for he was ever returning [in repentance to his Lord]!* (38:44).

They include glad tidings, blessings, and mercy, for God ﷻ has said: *And give glad tidings to those who are patiently enduring. to those who say, when a misfortune strikes them: "To God we belong, and to Him we are returning." Such are they on whom are blessings from their Lord, and mercy. Such are the rightly guided* (2:155-7). They include love from God ﷻ, for He has said: *God loves those who are patiently enduring* (3:146). They include the highest levels in the Garden of Paradise, for God ﷻ has said: *Those shall be awarded the highest heaven, for having endured with patience* (25:75). They include the tremendous honour, for God ﷻ has said: *Peace be upon you, because you endured with patience* (13:24). They also include a reward without limit and without end, far beyond the imaginings of creatures, their reckoning and their comprehension, for God ﷻ has said: *Surely the patiently enduring will be paid their wages in full without reckoning* (39:10).

Glory be to a Deity [*Ilāh*] who is a Noble Master! How Generous is He, for He bestows all these gracious favours on His servant, in this world and the Hereafter, in reward for the patience of an hour! It must now be clear to you that the benefit of this world and the Hereafter resides in patience. The Prophet ﷺ once said: "All that is good for the true believers resides in the patience of one hour." The poet spoke well when he said:

> Patience is the key to what is hoped for,
> and everything good is because of it,

so endure with patience, even if the nights are long,
  for the stubborn horse may then prove manageable,
and through patience you may find attainable
  what once made you say: "Alas, it will never be!"

Another poet said:

I endured with patience, and patience became part of my nature.
  Let it suffice you that God has commended patience!
I shall endure with patience, until God judges between us,
  whether it be a matter of ease, or a matter of difficulty.

You must therefore take advantage of this noble and praiseworthy virtue, and spare no effort in its constant practise, for then you may be numbered among the successful. God ﷻ is the Custodian of enabling grace!

You may ask: "What is the real meaning of patience, and what is its legal status?"

You should therefore know that, in classical Arabic, the term *ṣabr* [patience] is synonymous with *ḥabs* [confinement; restraint]. God ﷻ has said: *And restrain yourself along with those who cry unto their Lord in the morning and the evening, seeking His countenance; and do not let your eyes overlook them, desiring the pomp of the life of this world. And do not obey someone whose heart We have made heedless of Our remembrance, who follows his own lust and whose case has been abandoned* (18:28).

Patience [*ṣabr*] is attributed to God ﷻ, but only in the sense of restraint [*ḥabs*], since He restrains the torment from the sinful offenders, instead of inflicting it upon them immediately [in this world]. In relation to the endeavours of the heart, the term *ṣabr* is used because it signifies restraining the lower self from anguish [*jazaʿ*], and *jazaʿ*, according to some of the scholars, means expressing your perturbation in the face of adversity. Others maintain, however, that *jazaʿ* means seeking to escape from adversity without making the intention contingent on the will of God ﷻ, whereas *ṣabr* means refraining from it [from *jazaʿ* in the latter sense].

The stronghold of patience [*ṣabr*] is remembering the extent and the timing of adversity, that it will neither increase nor diminish, and that it will neither be brought forward nor postponed. There is no benefit in anguish [*jazaʿ*], but only harm and danger.

The stronghold of this stronghold is remembering the excellence of God's recompense for patience, and the generous favour that is held in store for it in His presence. God ﷻ is the Source of enabling grace!

§ REPELLING HINDRANCES

It is incumbent upon you to surmount this difficult and obstructive hurdle, by repelling these four hindrances [ʿawāriḍ] and removing their cause. If you fail to do so, they will not let you remember the worshipful service that is your goal. They will not allow you to think about it, let alone enable you to accomplish it. Each one of them presents a distracting preoccupation, in both the short term and the long term.

The most serious and problematic of them all is the business of sustenance [rizq] and its management. That is the greatest trial for the majority of people. It wearies their natural aptitudes, preoccupies their hearts, multiplies their cares, narrows their lives, and magnifies their liabilities and their burdens. It diverts them away from God ﷻ and His service, towards the service of this world and the service of creatures, so they live in this world in heedlessness and darkness, weariness and exhaustion, abasement and humiliation. They approach the Hereafter bankrupt, facing the reckoning and the torment, unless God ﷻ bestows His mercy through His gracious favour.

Notice how many a Qurʾānic verse [āya] God ﷻ has revealed on that subject [of sustenance], and how often He has mentioned His promise, His guaranty, and His oath concerning it. The prophets and the scholars have not ceased to admonish people and make them aware of the path. They have compiled books, coined allegories for them, and put them in fear of offending God ﷻ, yet, in spite of all that, they are not rightly guided, do not practise true devotion, and do not experience tranquillity. No indeed, they are plunged in a flood of anxious concern, constantly afraid of missing a lunch or a supper.

The root of all that is too little reflection on the signs of God ﷻ, too little meditation on the works of God ﷻ, failure to consider the speech of God's Messenger ﷺ, and failure to ponder the sayings of the righteous, combined with receptivity to the whisperings of the devil, listening to the speech of the ignorant, and being misled by the habits of the negligent. The devil thereby gains control of them, and bad habits take root in their hearts, so that reduces them to weakness of the heart and frailty of certitude.

As for the best of people, those who are endowed with faculties of discernment, and who are masters of earnest endeavour and dedicated striving, they clearly discern the path of Heaven, so they do not toy with the material means of the earth. They cling to the lifeline of God,[6] so they take no interest in the attachments of their fellow creatures. They are fully convinced by the signs of God ﷻ and they recognise His path, so they take no notice of the temptations of the devil, their fellow creatures, and the lower self. If a devil, a selfish instinct, or a person tempts them to do something, they engage the tempter in dispute, repudiation, and contradiction, until people turn away from them, the devil leaves them alone, the lower self submits to them, and the right path is straight ahead of them.

We are told that Ibrāhīm ibn Ad'ham (may God bestow His mercy upon him) was intending to enter the desert, when Satan came to him and tried to scare him, by saying: "This is a perilous desert, and you have no provision with you and no means [of survival]!" Ibrāhīm thereupon resolved (may God bestow His mercy upon him) that he would traverse the desert without that [provision for the journey], and that he would not traverse it without performing a thousand cycles of prayer beneath each and every milestone. He acted in accordance with his resolution, and stayed in the desert for twelve years. In one of those years, [the Caliph] ar-Rashīd went on the Pilgrimage [*Hajj*], and he saw Ibrāhīm praying beneath a milestone. He was told: "This is Ibrāhīm ibn Ad'ham, performing the ritual prayer," so he approached him and said: "How are you, O Abū Ishāq?" Ibrāhīm gave the poetic response:

> We patch this world of ours by shredding our religion,
>> so our religion does not last, and neither does what we patch.
> Congratulations to a servant who prefers God, his Lord,
>> and donates his worldly interest to whatever lies in store!

We are told that one of the righteous (may God bestow His mercy upon him) was in a certain desert, when Satan told him in a seductive whisper: "You are without provision, and this is a perilous desert, devoid of any cultivation and unpopulated." He thereupon resolved that he would travel in spite of his lack of provision, that he would follow the path without receiving anything from people, and that he would eat nothing until butter and honey were placed in his mouth. Then he turned aside from the main road, and went on his way.

He said (may God bestow His mercy upon him): "I traveled as God willed, and I came upon a caravan that had gone astray. When I saw the people in that caravan, I threw myself down on the ground, so that they would not notice me, but God ﷻ caused them to travel until they reached me. I closed my eyes as they approached me, and they said: "This is someone lost, who has fainted from hunger and thirst. Fetch some butter and some honey, and put them in his mouth. Perhaps he will recover consciousness!" They promptly fetched some butter and some honey, so I clenched my mouth and my teeth. Then they brought a knife, intending to use it to pry my mouth open, so I laughed and opened my mouth. When they saw me act like that, they said: 'Are you a lunatic?' I said: 'No, and praise be to God ﷻ!' I then told them something about what had happened to me with the devil, and they found that truly amazing."

According to one of our shaikhs (may God bestow His mercy upon them): "In the course of one of my journeys, I paused to spend days of learning in a mosque far removed from the populace. I was traveling without provision, in accordance with the custom of our saints, so the devil whispered to me: 'This is a mosque far distant from the populace. If you travel to a mosque in a populated area, its people will notice you and attend to your needs.' I said: 'I shall not break my journey anywhere but here. I am under oath to God ﷻ that I shall not eat anything except sweetmeat, and that I shall not eat that until it is put into my mouth, morsel by morsel.' I then performed the late evening prayer, and locked the door.

"When an early segment of the night had passed, I suddenly heard a person knocking on the door, and he was holding a lamp. Since the knocking went on and on, I opened the door, to find myself facing an old woman accompanied by a young man. She came inside and set before me a dish of sweet jelly, saying: 'This young man is my son. I prepared this sweet jelly for him, but an argument occurred between us, so he swore that he would not eat until a strange man ate with him.' (Or she may have said: 'This is the stranger who is in the mosque, so eat, and may God bestow His mercy upon you!') She then started putting a morsel into my mouth, and a morsel into her son's mouth, until we were satisfied.

The pair of them then departed, and I locked the door, while feeling amazed at what had happened."

Stories like this describe the dedicated strivings of the righteous, and their defiant opposition to the devil. That should contain three benefits for you:

1. You should understand that sustenance will not escape, in any case whatsoever, from someone for whom it has been predestined.

2. You should understand that the matter of sustenance and absolute trust [*tawakkul*] is very important indeed, and that the devil resorts to very sly tricks and temptations in this arena. Even the likes of those ascetic imāms [in the stories above] were not immune to that, and the devil did not despair of them. Even after those long spiritual exercises and the many dedicated efforts they had previously expended, they still needed to ward him off with these refutations. By my life, even if someone struggled against the lower self and the devil for seventy years, he could not feel sure that they would not tempt him, just as they tempt the novice in worshipful service. They would even tempt him as they tempt a heedless individual, who has never devoted an hour to spiritual exercise. Then, if they got the better of him, they would surely disgrace him and destroy him, with the destruction suffered by the heedlessly deluded. In that there is a warning for those endowed with faculties of discernment.

3. You should understand that the matter is not brought to completion, except through absolute commitment and the utmost endeavour, for they [those ascetic imāms] were just like you in flesh and blood and body and spirit. As a matter of fact, they were more fragile than you in body, weaker in limbs and organs, and more delicate in bones, but they had the strength of knowledge, the light of certitude, and aspiration in the matter of religion. This made them capable of such dedicated efforts, and of attaining to such high stations. You must therefore attend to your lower self. May God bestow His mercy upon you, and us, and may he cure it [the lower self] of this chronic disease, so that you may prosper, if God ﷻ so wills!

Now, after all that has been said above, I shall single out certain important items for your attention, since they will benefit the heart if you reflect on them. They will furnish you with the substance of this chapter, and leave you with a clear understanding of the truth, if you consider them carefully and put them into practise. God ﷻ is the Source of enabling grace.

1. You must know that God 🕮 has guaranteed sustenance for His servants in His Book. He has guaranteed your sustenance and pledged Himself to provide you with it. What would you say, if one of the kings of this world promised to welcome you as his guest at night, and to entertain you at dinner, assuming that you believed him to be truthful, so that he would not lie or break his promise? What would you say, for that matter, if you received such a promise from a commoner, or a Jew, or a Christian, or a Magian, who was apparently honest and sincere in what he said? Would you not rely on him and his promise, feel comfortable with what he said, and have no worry about your supper that night, because of your trust in him?

Well then, what do you think of the fact that God 🕮 has not only guaranteed your sustenance for you, and pledged Himself to provide it, but has solemnly sworn an oath to that effect in several places [in the Qur'ān]? How is it that you do not feel comfortable with His promise, that you do not rely on His word and His guaranty, that you pay no attention to His solemn oath, and that your heart is actually disturbed and ill at ease? What a disgrace, if only you could see its evil consequences! What a misfortune, if only you knew what it really means!

'Alī ibn Abī Ṭālib 🕮 is said to have uttered these poetic verses:

> Do you seek God's sustenance from someone other than Him,
>   and do you wake up feeling no fear of the consequences?
> Are you content with a money changer, even if he is a polytheist,
>   though you are not content with your Lord as a guarantor?
> It seems that you have not read what is in His Book,
>   so you have become extremely weak in certitude.

This attitude to the matter [of sustenance] is conducive to doubt and suspicion, and the person concerned is in danger—the refuge is with God!—of being deprived of true knowledge and religion. This is the context in which He said: *And put all your trust in God, if you are indeed believers* (5:23). *And in God let the believers put all their trust* (3:122). This single item is therefore sufficient for the believer who is seriously interested in the state of his religion. There is no might nor any power except with God, the All-High, the Almighty.

2. You must know that sustenance is foreordained. That is clearly stated in the Book of God 🕮 and the traditions of God's Messenger 🕮. You must also know that His foreordainment [*qisma*] does not alter and does not change. If you

refuse to acknowledge foreordainment, or accept the idea of its cancellation, you are knocking on the door of unbelief. (We take refuge with God!) If you know it to be a true fact that does not change, what can be gained from anxious concern and searching, except humiliation and degradation in this world, and agony and loss in the Hereafter? That is why the Prophet ﷺ once said: "[This is] the sustenance of so-and-so, the son of so-and-so" is inscribed on the back of the whale and the bull, so the greedy person gets nothing extra except trouble. Our own Shaikh (may God bestow His mercy upon him) had this to say on the subject: "Whenever something has been predestined for your pair of jaws, no one but you will ever chew it, so eat your sustenance—woe unto you!—with dignity, and do not eat it with shame." This item is also sufficient for real men.

3. I heard from my Shaikh, the Imām [al-Ḥaramain] (may God bestow His mercy upon him), that the Professor [Abū Isḥāq] (may God bestow His mercy upon him) used to say: "Concerning the matter of sustenance, I have found satisfaction in pondering and telling myself: 'Surely this sustenance is for life and livelihood, for the corpse does nothing with sustenance. The life of the servant is in the treasury of God ﷻ and at His disposal, and the same is true of sustenance: if He wills, He gives it to me, and if He wills, He withholds it from me. It is concealed from me, entrusted to God ﷻ, who manages it as He wills, and I am comfortable with that." This is a subtle item, sufficient for the masters of verification.

4. God ﷻ has guaranteed the servants' sustenance, but He has only guaranteed the sustenance that provides essential nourishment and growth, including physical stamina and preparation [for worshipful service].

§ THE MATERIAL MEANS OF SUSTENANCE

As for the material means of sustenance [*asbāb*], in the form of food and drink, if the servant devotes himself to the worshipful service of God ﷻ, and puts all his trust in Him, the material means may sometimes be withheld from him. He must not be concerned about that, however, and he must not be troubled by it, because the fact of the matter, as he well knows, is that the guaranty applies to support of the physical constitution. Absolute trust in God ﷻ is relevant only in this sense, not in any other, and this [support of the physical constitution] is what can be expected from God ﷻ. He will undoubtedly assist the servant to fulfil the duty of worship and service, so long as his term of life and his obligation to worship continue, for this is the purpose [for which He created His servant].

God ﷻ is capable of whatever He wills. If He so wills, He supports the physical constitution of His servant with food and drink, or with clay and soil, or with *tasbīḥ* [the glorification of God] and *tahlīl* [the affirmation that there is no god but God], as in the case of the angels. If He so wills, He uses some other means, different from all of these. The servant needs only the stamina and strength for worshipful service, not eating and drinking, the intensity of carnal desire and the enjoyment of pleasure. There is no reason, therefore, to be concerned about the means of sustenance.

This explains how the worshippers and ascetics found the strength to pursue their journeys, traveling by night and day. Some of them did not eat for ten days at a stretch, and some of them did not eat for a month or two months, yet they had the strength to carry on. Some of them used to swallow sand, which God ﷻ would convert into nourishment for them. For instance, in the case of Sufyān ath-Thawrī (may God bestow His mercy upon him), it is related that his funds ran out in Mecca, so he survived for fifteen days by swallowing sand. According to Abū Muʿāwiya al-Aswad: "I saw Ibrāhīm ibn Adʾham eating clay for twenty days." According to al-Aʿmash: "Ibrāhīm at-Taimī (may God bestow His mercy upon him) said to me: 'I have not eaten for a month.' I exclaimed: 'For a month?!' He said: 'It would have been two months, except that a person implored me by God ﷻ to accept a bunch of grapes, so I ate them, and now I am complaining about my stomach!'" You should not find any of that surprising, for God ﷻ has the power to do whatever He wills.

Consider the case of this invalid, who does not eat for a month, yet he stays alive, even though the invalid is inevitably weaker and more fragile in nature than someone who is strong and healthy. As for someone who dies of hunger, that is because his appointed term has arrived, as in the case of someone who dies of overeating and indigestion. I am told that Abū Saʿīd al-Kharrāz (may God bestow His mercy upon him) once said: "My relationship with God ﷻ was such that He would feed me once every three days, so I entered the desert and went for three days without eating any food. Then, on the fourth day, I felt weak, so I stayed sitting in my place. Suddenly, I heard an invisible caller crying: 'O Abu's-Saʿīd, which is dearer to you, a means of sustenance, or strong energies?' I said: 'Strong energies!' Then I stood up at once. Three days seemed like a very short time to me now, so I spent twelve days without eating, and I suffered no pain on that account."

As for the situation in which the servant experiences the withholding of the means of sustenance, and he knows how to put all his trust in God ﷻ, he must be firmly convinced that God ﷻ will support him with strength, so he must not be dismayed. It is his duty, in fact, to express his gratitude to God ﷻ by giving Him many thanks for that experience. God ﷻ has treated him with gracious favour and kindness, since He has relieved him of trouble and granted him assistance. Through that gift of grace, the servant has achieved the essential purpose and the goal, and God ﷻ has relieved him of the burden [of sustenance] and the indirect means [of obtaining it], ruptured the ties of custom for his sake, shown him the way of power, likened his state to the state of the angels, and raised him above the condition of animals and the common folk. You must therefore contemplate this great principle, so that you may gain vast profit, if God ﷻ so wills.

Perhaps you will say: "You have gone to excess in this subsection, violating the conciseness stipulated for the present book."

My response will be: By God's Everlasting Life, what I have included here is very little, compared with what is needed in this context, since it is most important in relation to worshipful service. Indeed, it is central to the whole subject of this world and servanthood. If someone has a serious interest in this subject, let him realise that and give it all the attention it deserves, for, unless he does so, he is missing the target.

If you need proof of the discernment of the scholars of the Hereafter and those who truly know God ﷻ, it is that they founded their business on absolute trust in God ﷻ, devotion to the worshipful service of God ﷻ, and the severance of all attachments. They compiled so many books and offered so much wise advice! God ﷻ sent them helpers from among the leaders and companions, to provide them with pure goodness, so long as they did not join one of the sects of the ascetic imāms known as the Karrāmiyya, for they built their doctrine on foundations that were not correct.

We did not cease to be worthy of honour, so long as we adhered to the path [*minhāj*] of our own imāms, graduating from our places of worship and our colleges, every time, either as a leader in knowledge, like Professor Abū Isḥāq [al-Isfarānī], Abū Ḥāmid [al-Isfarānī ash-Shāfiʿī], Abuʾṭ-Ṭayyib [aṭ-Ṭabarī], Ibn Fawrak [al-Isbahānī], our own Shaikh [Imām Abū Bakr al-Warrāq], and other chieftains like them, or as a champion of truth [*ṣiddīq*] in worshipful service, like Abū Isḥāq ash-Shīrāzī, Abū Saʿīd aṣ-Ṣūfī, Naṣr al-Maqdisī, and other such leaders distinguished in knowledge and abstinence.

[We did not cease to be worthy] until some of our hearts became weak, and we were sullied by some of those attachments that are more harmful than beneficial. It was then that matters deteriorated, aspirations retreated, blessings flew away, and joys and sweet delights departed, to the point where hardly anyone is likely to be sincere in his worship, or to obtain any knowledge and experience of reality. Whatever light beams from us now, it shines only from those who have kept to the path of our righteous predecessors and our earlier shaikhs, like al-Ḥārith al-Muḥāsibī, Muḥammad ibn Idrīs ash-Shāfiʿī, [Abū Ibrāhīm] al-Mazanī, Ḥarmala [at-Tajībī], and other leaders of the religion (may God bestow His mercy upon them all), for, as the poet said:

> They did not spend their days except in virtuous restraint,
> and for the love of their Master they found no substitute.
> They were the best, champions of Truth, models of sainthood,
> who made the Master of masters the target of their quest.
> From every one who patiently endured, the knot of patience was untied,
> but the days did not loosen any knot from their contract [with God].

We were kings in the early period of our history, but then we became subjects. We were knights on horseback, but then we became pedestrians. If only we would never be separated from the path! God ﷻ is the One to whom we appeal for help against misfortunes, and He is the One whom we implore, begging Him not to deprive us of this spark of life. He is indeed Munificent, Generous, Gracious, and Compassionate.

§ CONCERNING DELEGATION

As for delegation [*tafwīḍ*], there are two essential points for you to consider: 1. You should know that the exercise of choice is appropriate only for someone who is knowledgeable about affairs in all their aspects, both outwardly and inwardly, both in their present condition and in their eventual outcome. Otherwise, he risks choosing something bad and destructive, instead of something inherently good and beneficial. As you are surely aware, if you said to a bedouin, or a villager, or a keeper of sheep and goats: "Examine these dirhams [silver coins] for me, and sort out the good ones from the bad," he would not do that correctly. If you made the same request of a townsman who was not a money changer, the task would probably be just as difficult for him. Your only safe course, therefore, is to present those coins to the money changer, who is skilled in handling gold and silver, and who knows their peculiarities and their secret characteristics. As for the knowledge that embraces all affairs, from all directions, it is available only to God 🕮, the Lord of All the Worlds, so no one is entitled to the exercise of choice and management, except God 🕮, Alone without any partner. That is why He says (More Glorious is He than any other sayer): *Your Lord creates and chooses whatever He wills. They never have any choice* (28:68). Then He has said: *Your Lord knows what their breasts conceal and what they publish* (28:69).

It is related that one of the righteous was told by God 🕮: "Ask and you shall receive!" He was blessed with right guidance, so he said: "One who knows all aspects tells someone who is ignorant of all aspects: 'Ask and you shall receive!' What do I know about what is good for me? So I ask Him, saying: 'You choose for me!'"

2. Suppose a man told you: "I shall take charge of all your affairs and manage all your necessary interests, so delegate the whole business to me, and focus your attention on the matter that truly concerns you." Assume that you considered him the most knowledgeable of all the people of your time, the wisest, the strongest, the most compassionate, the most righteous, the most honest, and the most trustworthy. Would you not seize that opportunity and regard it as a tremendous blessing? Would you not feel the greatest sense of appreciation for him, and offer him the most abundant thanks and the finest praise? Then, if he chose for you something in which you did not recognise the benefit, instead of finding that disturbing, you would rely on his management and feel comfortable. You would understand that whatever he chose for you could only be

good, and whatever he saw fit for you could only be in your best interest, after you had entrusted the business to him, and he had guaranteed all that.

Well then, what keeps you from delegating the business to God 🕮, the Lord of All the Worlds? He is the One who manages the entire universe, from heaven to the earth, for He is the Most Knowledgeable of the knowledgeable, the Most Capable of the capable, the Most Merciful of the merciful, and the Richest of the rich. Given the brilliance of His knowledge and the excellence of His management, His choice on your behalf will surely transcend your knowledge and understanding, so you must focus your attention on the matter that concerns you in preparation for your life in the Hereafter. If His choice on your behalf has a mysterious aspect, which you do not comprehend, you must be content with that and feel comfortable with it, however it may be, for it is surely good and beneficial.

You will draw the right conclusions from all this, if God wills. God 🕮 is the source of enabling grace.

§ CONTENTMENT WITH DESTINY

As for contentment with destiny [ar-riḍā bi'l-qaḍā'], you must consider two essential points, to which nothing further need be added:

1. The benefit of contentment in the present and the future. As for its benefit in the present, it is freedom of the heart and relief from useless anxiety. That is why one of the ascetics (may God bestow His mercy upon him) once said: "Since destiny is a true fact, anxiety is redundant." According to the traditional report, the Prophet 🕮 said to Ibn Masʿūd 🕮: "Let your anxiety be very slight, for whatever has been predestined will come about, and whatever has not been predestined will not come to you." This Prophetic saying is comprehensive, conveying much valuable meaning in very few words.

As for the benefit of contentment in the future, it is the reward of God 🕮 and His good pleasure. God 🕮 has said that *He is well pleased with them, and they are well pleased with Him* (5:119). By contrast, discontent is fraught with anxiety, sorrow, and distress in the present, and with the burden of sin and punishment in the future. It has no benefit, since destiny's decree is effective, so it will not be cancelled by your anxiety and your discontent. As the poet said:

Whatever is decreed, O self, endure it with patience,
    and may you be safe from that which is not foreordained.
You must realise that what is predestined will come about
    for certain, regardless of whether or not you practise patience.

The intelligent person will not choose useless anxiety, combined with the burden of sin and punishment, instead of the heart's comfort and the reward of the Garden of Paradise!

2. Discontent is fraught with the dire threat of danger and injury, unbelief [*kufr*], and hypocrisy [*nifāq*], unless God 🕌 overtakes you [with His mercy]. Reflect on His saying: *But, by your Lord, they will not believe until they make you judge of what is in dispute between them and find within themselves no dislike of what you decide, and submit with full submission* (4:65).

He has thus denied their claim to belief, by solemnly swearing that belief is absent from those who are discontented, and who find within themselves a dislike of the decision of God's Messenger 🕌. What then is the condition of someone who is displeased with God's decree? According to a traditional report, God 🕌 says: "If someone is not content with My decree, if he is not patient with My tribulation, and if he is not grateful for My blessing, let him choose a deity [*ilāh*] apart from Me."

Someone said: "It is as if He is saying: 'This person will not be content with Me as a Lord, as long as he is displeased, so let him choose another lord, with whom he is content.'"

For the intelligent person, this [saying attributed to God] is the ultimate threat and warning. One of the righteous predecessors spoke the truth, when he was asked: "What is servanthood [*ʿubūdiyya*] and what is Lordship [*Rubūbiyya*]?" and he replied: "It is for the Lord to decree, and for the servant to be content." This means that if the Lord decrees, but the servant is not content, it is pointless to speak of servanthood and Lordship. You must consider this principle, and scrutinise yourself, for then you may be safe, with God's help and His enabling grace.

§   CONCERNING PATIENCE

As for patience [*ṣabr*], it is a bitter medicine and a blessed though distasteful potion. It procures every benefit and protects you from every harm. Since the medicine fits this description, the intelligent person forces the lower self to drink it and gulp it down. He chokes on its bitterness and its sharpness, but he says: "The bitterness of an hour is the comfort of a year."

As for the benefits procured by patience, you should know that patience is fourfold: (1) patience in worshipful obedience, (2) patience in abstaining from sinful disobedience, (3) patience in avoiding the excesses of this world, and (4) patience in enduring trials and misfortunes.

If someone endures the bitterness of patience, and practises patience in these four areas, he will attain to acts of obedience, to their stations of righteousness, and to their generous reward in the Hereafter. He will not lapse into acts of sinful disobedience, their afflictions in this world and their dire consequences in the Hereafter. He will not be tried by the search for this world, by preoccupation with it in the present, and by the consequence in the future. His recompense will not be lost because of the tribulation he had to suffer. By virtue of patience, he will thus attain to worshipful obedience, its noble stations and its reward. He will attain to righteousness, abstinence, and generous recompense and reward from God ﷻ. The full extent thereof is a matter known only to God ﷻ. As for protection from causes of harm, he will be relieved of the trouble and hardship of impatience in this world, first of all, then of its burden and punishment in the Hereafter.

If he is too weak to practise patience, and follows the path of anguish, he will forfeit every benefit, and every cause of harm will adhere to him. There are several possibilities: (1) He will lose the benefit of worshipful obedience, since he does not endure its hardship with patience, does not put it into practise, and lacks the patience to maintain it. (2) He lacks the patience to refrain from sinful disobedience, so he lapses into it, or to avoid extravagance, so he becomes preoccupied with it. (3) He fails to endure a misfortune with patience, so he is deprived of the reward for patience. (4) Perhaps he will multiply his anguish, to the point where he forfeits the recompense [for patience], so he will suffer two misfortunes, one being the loss of the thing [that made him feel anguish in the first place], and the other being the loss of the reward and recompense.

Someone said: "Lack of patience in enduring a misfortune is worse than the misfortune itself. What benefit is there in something that robs you of what you stand to gain, and does not restore to you what you have lost? If one of the two escapes you, try to make sure that the other does not escape you as well!"

We are told that ʿAlī 🕮 consoled a man by saying: "If you are patient, the decrees of destiny will befall you, and you will be rewarded, but if you are impatient, the decrees of destiny will befall you, and you will bear the burden of sin."

The gist of the matter is that you must detach the heart from its usual ties, and prevent the lower self from following its regular habits. This calls for absolute trust in God (Glorious is His Name), forsaking the management of affairs and delegating them to God 🕮, without knowing the secret concealed within them. You must restrain the lower self from discontent and from impatience, despite its tendency to rush in that direction. You must curb it with the reins of contentment, and by swallowing the drink of patience, despite its aversion to that treatment. This task is bitter, painful and hard to bear, but it is an effective procedure and a rightly guided method. It has a praiseworthy outcome, with fortunate and blessed results.

What would you say about a kind and wealthy father, if he prevented his dear son from eating a date or an apple, when the boy was sore-eyed, then handed him over to his harshly strict teacher, who confined him in his presence all day long, upset his feelings, and took him to the cupper to undergo a blood-letting operation, causing him pain and distress? Would you suppose that he withheld that fruit because of stinginess? How could that be, when he gives to strangers and treats them generously? Did he withhold it because of contempt for this son of his? How could that be, when he keeps everything he possesses in store for him? Did he intend to trouble and hurt him, out of hatred for the lad? How could that be, when the boy is the solace of his eye and the fruit of his heart, and it would worry him if a wind blew on his son? By no means! He acted as he did because he knew it to be in his son's best interest, and that this slight inconvenience would lead to an excellent result and enormous benefit [by curing his eye disease].

What would you say about a skilful, wise and loving physician, if he withheld a drink of water from a seriously ill patient, when the invalid was so thirsty that his liver was roasting, and made him drink a distasteful fruit juice, repugnant to his nature? Would you suppose that he was motivated by animosity and spite? By no means! His action was wise and beneficent, because he knew for certain that giving the invalid what he craved would damage him immediately and ruin him completely, whereas withholding that from him would result in his recovery and his survival.

You must therefore reflect with care, O man, if God 🕮 withholds from you a loaf of bread or a silver coin, since you know for certain that He possesses what you desire, that He can cause it to reach you, and that He is the Lord of generosity and gracious favour. He knows your condition, for nothing is hidden from Him, so there is no question of deficiency, inadequacy, concealment or stinginess [where He is concerned]. Exalted is He beyond all that, and Sanctified is He, for He is the Richest of the rich, the Most Powerful of the powerful, the Most Knowledgeable of the knowledgeable, and the Most Generous of the generous. You must therefore know for a fact that he would not withhold something from you, except in your best interest. How could it be otherwise, when He says: *He is the One who created for you all that is in the earth* (2:29)?

How could it be otherwise, when He is the One who has generously endowed you with knowledge of Him, with knowledge beside which this world in its entirety amounts to nothing? According the well-known traditional report, God 🕮 says: "I keep My friends away from the bounty of this world, just as I keep the herdsman who cares for his camels away from the puddles of dung."

When He tries you severely, you must therefore know for certain that He has no need of your trial and tribulation, that He knows your condition and sees your weakness, and that He treats you with kindness and compassion. You have surely heard the saying of the Prophet 🕮: "God 🕮 is More Compassionate with His servant than the tender mother with her child."

If you know this, you will understand that He would not inflict this unpleasant trial upon you, except in your best interest. You may be ignorant of its benefit, but He knows that full well. This explains why you see Him multiplying the trial and tribulation of His saints and His chosen friends, those who are the most distinguished of His servants. In the words of the Prophet 🕮: "When God 🕮 loves a set of people, He tries them." And, "The people most severely tried are the prophets, then the martyrs, then the worthiest and the worthiest...."

If you see God withholding this world from you, and inflicting more and more hardships and suffering upon you, you must therefore know that you are noble in His sight, that you hold a lofty rank in His presence, and that He is making you tread the path of His saintly friends, for He sees you and He does not need that [withholding of this world...]. You have surely heard His saying: *So wait patiently for your Lord's decree, for you are surely in Our sight* (52:48).

You must acknowledge the gracious favour He bestows upon you, by looking after your best interest, multiplying your recompense and your reward, and appointing you to the ranks of the righteous and those who are distinguished in His sight. You will discover so many praiseworthy results and noble gifts! God is the Custodian of helpful guidance, through His favour and His grace.

§ SUMMARY OF HINDRANCES

In summary, if you know for certain that God ﷻ is the Guarantor of your sustenance, which you need for your survival and your performance of His worshipful service, that He is Capable of what He wills however He wills, and that He is aware of your need in every situation and at every moment, you will put all your trust in His true guaranty, and His genuine promise. Your heart will feel at ease with that, and you will forget about worldly attachments and material means, and your heart's addiction to them.

Worldly attachments do not enrich you or suffice you, without God ﷻ, for He is the One who makes it easy for you to eat and drink. It is He who makes your food and drink wholesome and enjoyable. It is He who supplies you with their energy and benefit, and protects you from their heaviness and harmfulness. He may also enrich you and suffice you without them, if He wills. The whole business depends on Him, Alone without any partner, so put all your trust in Him, not in any other.

You must likewise leave the management of your affairs to the One who manages the heavens and the earth. You must rid yourself of concern about anything beyond your knowledge, and of thinking about tomorrow's business. You must stop wondering whether something will happen tomorrow, or whether it will not happen, and how it will be [if it does happen]. You must stop saying "perhaps..." and "if...," since there is nothing in that except worrying the heart and wasting time. Maybe things will unfold in ways you never imagined, so that all your previous thinking and planning will prove to be a waste of precious time, nothing but a useless game. Worse still, you may suffer a loss that you sorely regret, for your heart may become preoccupied with it, and you may waste your whole life in the process. One of the pious ascetics ﷺ gave this poetic admonition:

The ordainments of God [al-Ilāh]
  and His judgement are predetermined,
so relieve your heart of "perhaps..." and "if...."

Another said:

Whatever is going to happen will happen in its own time,
  yet the brother of ignorance is worried and sorrowful,
for perhaps what he fears will never come to be,
  and perhaps what he hopes for will never happen.

In short, you must say to yourself: *"Nothing will ever befall us except what God has decreed for us. He is our Protecting Friend"* (9:51).

He is Sufficient for us, and excellent is the Custodian, since He is Powerful with no end to His Power, Wise with no end to His Wisdom, Compassionate with no end to His Compassion. Since He possesses these attributes, He deserves to receive all your trust, and to have the whole business delegated to Him. Delegation [tafwīd] is therefore incumbent upon you. You must likewise convince your heart that whatever God ﷻ has decreed, and whatever He decrees for you, is most appropriate and most beneficial, even if the nature thereof is a mystery beyond our knowledge.

You must also tell yourself: "Whatever is predestined will undoubtedly come to be, so there is no benefit in discontent. You have no choice in what God ﷻ does, so it is pointless to be displeased. Do you not say: 'I am well pleased with God ﷻ as a Lord'? So how can you not be content with His decree, when the decree is part of the business of Lordship and its privilege?! Contentment [ridā] is therefore incumbent upon you."

In similar fashion, when a misfortune befalls you and you experience something unpleasant, you must persuade your lower self to view it from the right perspective, and calm your heart so that it does not become perturbed. You must not succumb to complaining and impatient agitation, especially at the first shock. That is the crucial moment, when the lower self tends to react at great speed with habitual impatience, so you must tell it: "This misfortune has already occurred, so there is no expedient to ward it off." God ﷻ has prevented a much greater misfortune, for there are many kinds of trial and tribulation in His storehouses. This one will soon be over, so it will not last forever. It is a cloud that will surely disperse, so resign yourself to patience for a little while, for you will derive prolonged happiness from that.

You will receive a generous reward, once you have understood that there is no way of preventing what is destined to befall, that there is no benefit in impatient agitation, and that there no misfortune, in actual fact, in the presence of equanimity and patience. You must therefore occupy your tongue with *istirjā* [saying: "We belong to God, and to Him we are all returning (*innā li'llāhi wa innā ilaihi rājiʿūn*)"], and your heart with remembering the reward you will receive from God ﷻ. You must also remember how patiently the most terrible misfortunes were endured by those possessed of constancy [*ulu 'l-ʿazm*], meaning the prophets and the saintly friends of God ﷻ.

If this world is withheld from you for a time, you must tell your lower self: "He knows the situation best, and He is Most Compassionate with you and Most Generous. He is the One who feeds the dog in spite of its vileness, and feeds the unbeliever in spite of his hostility. I am His servant, acknowledging His Lordship and affirming His Oneness, so am I not worth a loaf of bread in His sight?! This is inconceivable, so recognise the fact that He has not withheld this world from you except for some enormous benefit. As He has said: God *will surely grant ease after hardship* (65:7).

Be patient for a little while, for then you will see the marvellous refinement of His work. You have surely heard the saying of the poet:

> Wait for the work of your Lord, for it will bring
> > what you desire in the form of relief near at hand,
> and do not despair, if nothing special has yet occurred,
> > for there are so many wondrous marvels in the Unseen.

Another poet said, in similar vein:

> O man beset with care,
> > if hardship affects you severely,
> you must think of: "Did We not expand....."[7]
> > Then hardship will come between two easements,

if you repeat [the *Sūra*],
    so be happy!

If you take these admonitions to heart, as well as others like them, and make a regular practise of repeating them, that will soon ease your hardships for you, provided you have a lofty aspiration and a serious dedication.

You have now learned how to protect yourself from these four hindrances, and obtained complete relief from the trouble they cause. In the sight of God ﷻ you have come to be one of those who put all their trust in Him, who delegate their affairs to Him, who are content with His decree, and who patiently endure His trial and tribulation. You have gained comfort of heart and body in this world, splendid reward and treasure in the Hereafter, and magnificent worth and affection in the sight of the Lord of All the Worlds. You have thus acquired the best of both abodes. The path of worshipful service lies straight ahead of you, since there is no impediment and no distraction. You have now surmounted this difficult hurdle!

We beseech God ﷻ to support you, and us, with the blessing of His enabling grace, for the whole business is at His disposal, and He is the Most Merciful of the merciful. There is no might nor any power except with God, the All-High, the Almighty.

THE HURDLE OF INCENTIVES

IT IS NOW incumbent upon you, O my brother, to travel ahead, since the path lies straight before you, the way has been made easy, the impediments have been removed, and the hindrances have disappeared. In order to travel the straight path, you have no option but to feel both fear and hope, and to persist in experiencing their true significance to the fullest extent.

§ CONCERNING FEAR

In the case of fear [*khawf*], there are two reasons for clinging to it:

1. Deterrence from sinful acts of disobedience. This lower self that is always instigating evil [*an-nafs al-ammāra*] is strongly disposed towards wickedness, constantly looking for trouble. It will not desist from that, unless it receives a tremendously fear-inspiring shock and an extremely intimidating threat. It is not free [from slavery], so it is not concerned about loyalty and restrained from offensive conduct by a sense of shame. As the poet said:

> The slave is thrashed with the stick,
> while blame is enough for the freeman.

To manage the lower self, you must thrash it with the whip of intimidation, in word and deed and thought. We are told that the lower self of one of the righteous tempted him to commit an act of sinful disobedience, so he went and stripped off his clothes, rolled in the sun-baked dust, and said to his lower self: "Taste [the hot dust], for the Fire of Hell is far hotter than this!" Yes indeed, the lower self is a corpse by night and an idle mischief-maker by day.

2. The servant must not take pride in acts of worshipful obedience, for he will perish if he does so. He must curb the lower self with blame and criticism, finding fault with its vices and sins, which contain all sorts of dangers. It is reported that the Prophet ﷺ once said: "If Jesus and I were taken to task for what these two [lower selves of ours] have earned, we would suffer a torment suffered by no other creature." And he pointed with two of his fingers [to represent each of their lower selves].

We are told that al-Ḥasan [al-Baṣrī] used to say: "Not one of us is safe from having committed a sin, so the door of forgiveness may be locked in his face, for he acts in a way that is improper."

Ibn al-Mubārak used to say, while rebuking his lower self: "You talk like the pious ascetics, but you act like the hypocrites, and you long for the Garden of Paradise. Alas and alack! Another set of people are entitled to the Garden of Paradise, for they perform deeds quite different from those you perform."

These admonitions, and others like them, are examples of how the servant must rebuke the lower self, and scold it repeatedly, so that it will not take pride in an act of worshipful obedience, or commit an act of sinful disobedience. God ﷻ is the source of enabling grace!

§ CONCERNING HOPE

As for hope [rajā'], you must maintain the feeling of it for two reasons:

1. It provides an incentive to acts of worshipful obedience. That is because goodness is a heavy burden. The devil tries to deter you from it, and passion invites you to its opposite. The state of the heedless, who constitute the majority of people, is obviously a natural disposition to gratify the lower self. The reward for acts of obedience is out of their sight, and the distance to its achievement

seems very remote to them. This being the case, the lower self feels no incentive to goodness, and has no desire to accord it the respect it deserves.

If anything can make the lower self interested in goodness, it must be something that matches and equals these obstacles, or rather outweighs them. That something is strong hope for the mercy of God ﷻ, and intense longing for the blessing of His reward and His noble recompense. According to our own Shaikh (may God bestow His mercy upon him): "Sadness prevents the consumption of food. Fear prevents sins. Hope reinforces acts of worshipful obedience. The remembrance of death leads to abstinence from excess."

2. Hope makes it easier for you to bear difficulties and hardships. If someone truly understands what he is seeking, he finds it easy to make the necessary effort. If someone is pleased by something, and feels a genuine longing for it, he readily endures the difficulty involved, and thinks nothing of the trouble he encounters in its pursuit. If a person loves someone with genuine affection, he also loves to endure the ordeal his loved one imposes, to the point where he discovers all kinds of delight in that ordeal.

Consider how the beekeeper thinks nothing of the stings inflicted by the bees, because the sweetness of the honey is fresh in his memory. Consider the hired workman, who cares nothing about climbing that tall ladder with a heavy load, throughout the long, hot summer day, because he remembers that he is due to collect a couple of silver coins in the evening. Consider the peasant farmer, who does not let his thinking dwell on the harshness of the heat and the cold, and the year-long drudgery and toil out in the fields, because he remembers the time of produce on the threshing floor.

Consider likewise, O my brother, those worshipful servants who are committed to dedicated striving, for they remember the Garden of Paradise, that delightful place of rest with its many kinds of comfort, including its dark-eyed maidens [*ḥūr*], its palaces, its food and drink, its ornaments and fine clothes, and everything else that God ﷻ has prepared for its inhabitants. They find it easy to bear any toil involved in worshipful service, or the loss of any pleasure and enjoyment in this world, or anything they suffer in the form of injury, humiliation, affliction or adversity, for the sake of the Garden of Paradise.

It is related that the companions of Sufyān ath-Thawrī ؓ once told him what they thought about his fear, his dedicated striving, and the shabbiness of his outer condition. They said: "O teacher, even if you reduced this strenuous exertion, you would still reach your intended goal, if God ﷻ so willed." Sufyān said: "How can I fail to strive with dedicated effort, when I have heard that the people of the Garden of Paradise will be in their places, and a light will appear to them, illuminating the eight Gardens. They will suppose that light comes from the Lord ﷻ, so they will fall down in prostration. Then they will hear the call: 'Raise your heads! It is not what you suppose. It is merely the light of a young woman, smiling in the face of her husband.'" Sufyān then recited these poetic verses:

> He whose abode is Paradise will not be harmed
> > by any wretchedness or poverty that he must bear.
> See how he walks sadly, in fear and in dread,
> > walking to the mosques in tatters and rags.
> O lower self, how patiently can you endure a flame?
> > The time is near when you must advance after retreating.

The business of servanthood hinges on two things: the performance of worshipful obedience, and the avoidance of sinful disobedience. None of that can be achieved, however, in the company of this lower self that is always instigating evil [*an-nafs al-ammāra bi's-sū'*], except through inducement and intimidation, inspiring hope and instilling fear. The stubborn mule needs a leader to lead it, and a driver to drive it. If it falls into a danger spot, it may need to be beaten with a whip from one side, and offered barley from another side, until it gets up and moves away from whatever it fell into. The delinquent youth will not attend school classes, without inducement from his parents and intimidation from the teacher.

This lower self is likewise a stubborn mule that has stumbled into the pitfall of this world, so fear is its whip and its driver, while hope is its barley and its leader. It is the delinquent youth, who must be moved to attend the classes of worship and righteousness, so its intimidation is the reminder of the Fire of Hell and the punishment [of the Hereafter], and its inducement is the reminder of the Garden of Paradise and its reward.

For the servant who seeks worshipful service and spiritual training, it is likewise necessary to make the lower self conscious of two feelings, they being fear and hope. Otherwise, the unruly lower self will not assist him in that endeavour. For this reason, [the Qur'ān, which God ﷻ has called] the Wise Remembrance [*adh-Dhikr al-Ḥakīm*][8] has coupled the promise [*waʿd*] and the threat [*waʿīd*], meaning the inducement and the intimidation, and has laid great stress on both of them. It has described the noble reward in terms that make its forfeiture unbearable, and described the painful punishment in terms that make its agony intolerable. You must therefore maintain these two feelings [fear and hope], for then you will achieve your goal of worshipful service, and the endurance of hardship will become easy for you. God 🕮 is the Custodian of helpful guidance, through His grace and His mercy.

You may ask: "What is the real meaning of hope and fear, and what is their classification?"

You must therefore know that, according to our scholars (may God bestow His mercy upon them), fear and hope fall into the same category as *khawāṭir* [spontaneous feelings; random notions], and the servant is only obliged to cultivate their stimulants. Our scholars have said: "Fear [*khawf*] is a shudder that occurs in the heart, in reaction to an unpleasant thought. Dread [*khashya*] is almost synonymous, but it implies a kind of reverential awe. The opposite of fear is boldness [*jarā'a*], but it may also be contrasted with the sense of security [*amn*]. The adjectives *khā'if* [fearful, afraid] and *āmin* [secure] correspond to the nouns *khawf* [fear] and *amn* [security]. The *āmin* is someone who is bold in relation to God 🕮. Boldness [*jarā'a*] is therefore the true opposite of fear."

The stimulants of fear are four in number: (1) Remembering the many sins that have previously been committed, and the multitude of victims who have accused the wrongdoer, while you are in suspense, for the means of redemption is not yet clear to you; (2) remembering the severity of God's punishment, which you lack the strength to bear; (3) remembering that your lower self is too weak to endure the punishment; and (4) remembering that God 🕮 has the power to deal with you whenever He wills and however He wills.

As for hope [*rajā'*], it is the heart's delight in the knowledge of God's gracious favour, and its happiness with the abundance of God's mercy. This kind of hope is included in the category of spontaneous feelings [*khawāṭir*], so it has not been ordained for the servant. Another kind of hope has been ordained for the servant, and that is remembering the gracious favour of God 🕮, His abundant generosity and His mercy. The term *rajā'* is also applied to the intention that is made contingent on God's will.

Our present subject is the first kind of hope, which is the feeling of delight and happiness. Its opposite is despair, which is the sense of losing God's mercy and His gracious favour, and the heart's detachment from that feeling. Such despair is a sinful act of sheer disobedience. This kind of hope must be a strict duty [*fard*], if the servant has no other means of guarding against despair. If he does have other means, it is a supererogatory duty [*nafl*], additional to the general belief in God's gracious favour, His abundant generosity and His mercy.

The stimulants of hope are also four in number:

1. Remembering the gracious favours that God ﷻ has previously bestowed upon you, without any action [on your part] or any intercessor [on your behalf].

2. Remembering what God ﷻ has promised, as your share of His plentiful reward and His enormous favour, commensurate with His abundant grace and His noble generosity, and that your entitlement thereto does not depend on your action, since, if it did depend on your action, it would be a lesser thing and a smaller matter.

3. Remembering the abundance of God's blessing, conferred on you in your religion and your worldly life, at the present time, in the form of all kinds of support and kindnesses, without any claim to entitlement or any request [on your part].

4. Remembering the vast extent of God's mercy, that His mercy has outstripped His wrath, and that He is the All-Merciful, the All-Compassionate, the Independent, the Generous, the One who is Kind to His believing servants.

If you are diligent in practising these two kinds of remembrance, that will lead you to conscious awareness of fear and hope in every situation. God ﷻ is the Custodian of helpful guidance, through His grace and His favour.

§ TWO PATHS OF DANGER

It is therefore incumbent upon you to surmount this hurdle with perfect caution and circumspection, and with the utmost care, for it is a hurdle precarious to tackle and hazardous to cross. That is because its path lies between two perilous and dangerous paths, one being the path of [false] security and the other the path of despair. The path of hope and fear is the just path between the two unjust paths. If hope prevails upon you, so that you lose fear altogether, you will slip onto the path of [false] security. *No one feels secure from God's devising, except those folk who are losers* (7:99). If fear prevails upon you, so that you lose hope altogether, you will slip onto the path of despair. *No one despairs of God's Spirit, except the unbelieving folk* (12:87). If you ride between fear and hope, and cling to them both together, that is the just and straight path, the way of God's saints and His chosen friends, whom God ﷻ has described in His saying: *They used to vie with one another in good deeds, and they cried to Us in longing and in fear, and they were submissive unto Us* (21:90).

If three paths become apparent to you in this hurdle: (1) the path of [false] security and boldness, (2) the path of despair and hopelessness, and (3) the path of fear and hope, stretched out between them, and if you take a step away from it [the middle path] to your right or your left, you will slip onto one of the two deadly paths, and perish with those who perish.

Furthermore, the fact is that the two unjust and deadly paths are wider and more spacious, more attractive and easier to tread than the just path. If you look from the side of [false] security, you will see the vast extent of God's mercy, the abundance of His grace and the profusion of His generosity, to the point where no fear remains with you. You will therefore put all your trust in that, immediately, and you will feel secure. If you look from the side of fear, you will see the might of God's power and authority, the greatness of His awesome dignity, the precision of His commandment and the meticulousness of His reckoning, in relation to His saints and His chosen friends, to the point where hope will scarcely remain with you, so you will promptly despair.

This means that you should not look only at the vastness of God's mercy, to the point where you become completely trusting and feel secure, and that you should not look only at His awesome dignity and meticulous reckoning, to the point where you despair. You should rather look at the former and the latter together, and take something from each. Then you must ride a narrow path between them, and stick to that path, so that you will be truly safe. The path of absolute hope is easy, broad and wide, and its ultimate outcome will bring you to false security and loss. The path of absolute fear is also broad and wide, and its ultimate outcome will bring you to error. Between the two lies the just path, by which I mean the path of fear and hope. Even if it is a narrow and difficult path, it is a safe road and a clear route, leading to forgiveness and beneficence, then to the Gardens and Riḍwān [the keeper of Paradise], and to meeting the Sovereign All-Merciful ﷻ. You have surely heard His statement about the sons of this road: *They call on their Lord in fear and hope* (32:16).

He then went on to say: *So no soul knows what comfort is kept secretly in store for them, as a reward for what they used to do* (32:17).

You must consider all this with very great care, make ready for action, and pay close attention to the task, for it will not come easily. God is the Custodian of enabling grace!

You must also know that it will not be a simple matter for you to tread this path, to force this obstinate lower self, with its lazy attitude to goodness, to abstain from what it dearly loves, and to perform the acts of obedience that weigh so heavily upon it. Progress depends on the strict observance of three essentials, and on keeping them constantly in mind, without a break and without a moment of heedlessness: (1) Remembering the sayings of God (Exalted is He and Glory be to Him) concerning encouragement and intimidation. (2) Remembering His actions relating to punishment and pardon. (3) Remembering His recompense for His servants, in the form of reward and chastisement in the Hereafter.

Many pages are needed to explain each of these essential points in detail, so we have compiled a book devoted to them, entitled: *The Awakening of the Heedless* [*Tanbīh al-Ghāfilīn*]. In this present book, we shall provide quotations to help you achieve the goal, if God so wills. God is the Custodian of enabling grace!

§ FIRST ESSENTIAL: STATEMENTS OF GOD ﷻ

You must turn, O man, to the Glorious Book, and contemplate the verses [*āyāt*] concerning encouragement and intimidation, the inspiring of hope and the instilling of fear. The verses of hope include His saying:

Do not despair of the mercy of God; surely God forgives sins altogether. (39:53)

Who forgives sins but God. (3:135)

[God is] the Forgiver of sin, the Accepter of repentance? (40:3)

He is the One who accepts repentance from His servants, and pardons evil deeds. (42:25)

Your Lord has prescribed for Himself mercy. (6:54)

And My mercy embraces all things, so I shall prescribe it for those who are truly devout. (7:156)

To human beings, God is surely Ever-Gentle, All-Compassionate. (22:65)

And to the believers He is All-Compassionate. (33:43)

These, and others like them, are the verses of hope [*āyāt ar-rajā'*].

The verses of fear and stricture [*āyāt al-khawf wa 's-siyāsa*] include His saying:

O My servants, so beware of Me! (39:16)

What, did you suppose that We had created you for idle sport, and that you would not be returned to Us? (23:115)

What, does the human being suppose that he will be left to wander aimlessly? (75:36)

It will not be in accordance with your desires, nor the desires of the People of the Book. He who does something wrong will have the recompense thereof, and he will not find against God any protecting friend or helper. (4:123)

Yet they reckon that they do good work. (18:104)

And there will appear to them, from their Lord, that wherewith they never reckoned. (39:47) *And We shall advance upon the work they have done, and make it into scattered particles of dust.* (25:23)

We beg God ﷻ to save us by His mercy!

The fine verses that combine both fear and hope include His saying: *Announce to My servants that I am the All-Forgiving, the All-Compassionate.* (15:49)—which He followed immediately with: *And that My torment is the painful doom.* (15:50) —so that hope would not take charge of you completely. God ﷻ described Himself as: *The Stern in punishment* (40:3). Then He added immediately: *The Bountiful. There is no god but He* (40:3). This so that fear would not take charge of you completely. Even more surprising is His saying: *And God warns you to beware of Himself* (3:30), which He followed immediately with: *And God is Kind and Gentle with His servants* (3:30). More surprising than this is His saying: *If some-one fears the All-Merciful in secret....* (50:33), for He has linked fear to the Name "the All-Merciful" [*ar-Raḥmān*], not to another of His Names, such as "the All-Compelling" [al-Jabbār], "the Avenger" [al-Muntaqim], or "the All-Sublime" [al-Mutakabbir]. He has done so to connect fear with mercy, so that fear will not overwhelm your heart completely. The instilling of fear is thus accompanied by a reassuring and calming influence, as when you say: "You must surely be afraid of offending the tender-hearted mother!" "You must surely be afraid of offending the kind father!" "You must surely beware of offending the noble commander!" The purpose of that is to strike a fair balance, so that you do not swing towards false security or despair.

May God 🕮 include you, and us, among those who cultivate this wise remembrance, and who act upon it through His mercy! He is the Generous, the Noble One. There is no might nor any power except with God, the All-High, the Almighty.

§ SECOND ESSENTIAL: ACTS OF GOD 🕮

As for the aspect of fear, you must know that Iblīs worshipped God 🕮 for eighty-thousand years. It is said that he never stepped away from a spot, without first performing an act of prostration before God 🕮 in that place. Then he disobeyed one commandment [to prostrate himself before Adam], so God 🕮 expelled him from His door, wiped eighty-thousand years of worship from his face, cursed him till the Day of Doom, and prepared for him a painful torment, lasting for all eternity.

According to traditional report, the truthful and trustworthy [Prophet Muḥammad] 🕮 once saw Gabriel 🕮 clinging to the curtains of the Kaʿba, while screaming and shouting [in fear]: "My God and my Master! Do not change my name, and do not alter my body!"

As for Adam 🕮, His chosen friend and His Prophet, whom He created with His hand, before whom He made the angels prostrate themselves, and whom He transported on their necks into His vicinity, he lived in comfort [in the Garden of Paradise], but then he ate a single morsel for which he had not been granted permission, so he heard the call: "If someone disobeys Me, he will surely not be My neighbour!" God ﷻ then summoned the angels who carried Adam's couch, and commanded them to hurl him down from heaven to heaven, until they dropped him on the earth. According to traditional report, God ﷻ did not accept Adam's repentance, so he wept over that [act of disobedience he had committed] for two hundred years. He suffered the humiliation and tribulation that he suffered, and his offspring were left with the dire consequences of that [sin of his] for all eternity.

As for Noah, the Shaikh of the Envoys ﷺ, who endured what he endured for the sake of his religion, he spoke just a single word that was out of place, so he heard the call: *So do not ask of Me that whereof you have no knowledge. I admonish you, lest you be among the ignorant* (11:46).

According to some of the traditional reports, he did not raise his head heavenwards for forty years, due to his sense of shame before God ﷻ.

As for Abraham ﷺ, God's Bosom Friend [*Khalīlu 'llāh*], he committed only one mistake. He felt terribly afraid, so made the humble entreaty: *And Who, I ardently hope, will forgive me my sin on the Day of Doom* (26:82).

It is related that he wept from the intensity of fear, so God ﷻ sent him the trustworthy Gabriel ﷺ, who said to him: "O Abraham, have you ever seen a bosom friend torment his bosom friend with fire?" Abraham replied: "O Gabriel, if I remember my mistake, I shall forget His bosom friendship!"

As for Moses ﷺ, the son of ʿImrān, he was guilty of delivering one slap out of anger. He felt terribly afraid, so he humbled himself and sought forgiveness, saying: *"My Lord, I have wronged myself, so forgive me!"* (28:16).

As for Baʿlām ibn Bāʿūrāʾ, who lived in the time of Moses ﷺ, he was remarkable in that, when he looked towards the sky, he would see the Heavenly Throne [ʿArsh]. He is the person referred to in God's saying: *Recite to them the tale of him to whom We gave Our signs, but he sloughed them off* (7:175).

His only offence was that he showed a predilection for this world and its people, on one occasion, and omitted a single mark of respect for one of God's saintly friends. God ﷻ therefore stripped him of his knowledge and understanding, and compared him to the dog that is chased away, for He said: *His likeness is therefore as the likeness of the dog; if you attack him, he pants with his tongue out, and if you leave him, he pants with his tongue out. Such is the likeness of the people who deny Our signs. So narrate to them the story, for then they may reflect* (7:176).

Bal'ām's offence thus plunged him into the sea of error and perdition, for all eternity. I have even heard one of the scholars say: "At the beginning of his career, he was so remarkable that twelve thousand inkwells were provided in his classroom, for the students who took notes from him. Then he became outstanding as the first to compile a book, in which he stated that the universe has no creator." We take refuge with God ﷻ [from that blasphemy]! Then we take refuge with God ﷻ from His displeasure, from His painful torment, and from His disappointment, which we have no strength to endure. Consider the wickedness of this world and its evil, especially in its impact on the scholars, wake up and take heed, for the matter is perilous, life is short, too little work is done, and the Critic is Perceptive. If He sets the seal of goodness on our deeds, and pardons our mistakes, that is not difficult for Him.

As for David ﷺ, God's deputy [*khalīfa*] on His earth, he committed one sin, so he wept over that, until his tears caused grass to sprout on the ground. He said: "My God, will You not have mercy on my weeping and my humble entreaty?" He received the reply: "O David, you have forgotten your sin, but you have remembered your weeping!" God ﷻ did not accept his repentance for forty days, or, some say, for forty years.

As for God's Prophet Jonah ﷺ, he was guilty of one inappropriate burst of anger, so God ﷻ imprisoned him in the belly of the whale, beneath the depth of the oceans for forty days, while he cried: *"There is no god but You. Glory be to You! I have been one of the wrongdoers"* (21:87).

The angels heard his voice, so they said: "Our God and our Master, a familiar voice from a place unknown!" God ﷻ said: "That is the voice of My servant, Jonah," so the angels interceded on his behalf. Then, in spite of all that, He changed his name [to Dhu 'n-Nūn], for He said: And Dhu 'n-Nūn (21:87)— and thereby linked him to his prison [since Dhu 'n-Nūn means "Occupant of the Whale"]. Then God ﷻ said: *And the big fish swallowed him while he was blameworthy. And had he not been one of those who glorify [the Lord], he would have tarried in its belly until the day when they are resurrected* (37:142–44)

Then He mentioned His blessing and His gracious favour, for He said: *Had there not overtaken him a blessing from his Lord, he would have been cast upon the wilderness, while he was reprobate* (68:49).

You must contemplate this stricture, O miserable wretch!

Let us now move forward in time to the Chief of the Envoys, the most noble of God's creatures, to whom He said: *So tread the straight path as you are commanded, and those who turn [to God] with you, and do not transgress. He is All-Seeing of what you do* (11:112).

The Prophet 鬒 used to say: Hūd [the 11th Sūra of the Qur'ān] and its sisters have made my hair turn grey! It is said that he was referring to this verse [āya] and others like it in the Qur'ān, for God 鬒 said: *And ask forgiveness for your sin* (40:55)—until God 鬒 bestowed forgiveness upon him, and said: *And We have relieved you of your burden, that weighed down your back* (94:2,3).

He also said: *That God may forgive you your former and your latter sins* (48:2). After that, the Prophet 鬒 used to pray throughout the night, until his feet became swollen, so they would ask him: "Why do you still do this, O Messenger of God, when God has already forgiven you your former and your latter sins?" He would reply: "Am I not a grateful servant?" He would also say 鬒: "If Jesus and I were taken to task for what these two [lower selves of ours] have earned, we would suffer a torment suffered by no other creature."

He used to pray throughout the night, and he would weep and say: "I take refuge with Your pardon from Your punishment, and with Your good pleasure from Your displeasure! I take refuge with You from You! I cannot praise You as well as You have praised Yourself!"

As for the Companions, the best of a generation and the best of a community, they used to indulge in a certain amount of frivolity, so this saying of God 鬒 was sent down: *Is not the time now ripe for the hearts of those who believe to be humbled to the Remembrance of God and to the Truth which He has sent down, and that they do not become like those who received the Book of old, but the term was prolonged for them, and so their hearts were hardened, and many of them are profligates* (57:16).

God 鬒 then imposed strict rules and regulations and proprieties on this [Islamic] Community, despite the fact that it is blessed with merciful compassion, so that Yūnus ibn ʿUbaid used to say: "Since He has prescribed the amputation of a member of your body [your hand], as the penalty for stealing five silver coins, you cannot be sure that His torment tomorrow [in the Hereafter] will not be similar!" We beseech God ﷻ, the Compassionate, the Generous, imploring Him not to treat us with anything but His pure generosity. He is the Most Merciful of the merciful.

As for the aspect of hope, you must speak freely about God's abundant mercy. Who knows its full extent? Who knows its true quality and its utmost limit? He is the One who pardons seventy years of unbelief in exchange for an hour of belief. God ﷻ has said: *Tell those who disbelieve that, if they desist, that which is past will be forgiven them* (8:38).

Consider the case of Pharaoh's sorcerers, who came to fight Moses ﷺ, and who swore by the might of Pharaoh, his enemy. What actually happened was that they witnessed the miraculous sign of Moses ﷺ, so they acknowledged the Truth and they cried: *"We believe in the Lord of All the Worlds!"* (26:47).

There is no mention of their having adopted any practise in addition to this [affirmation of belief], but notice how often God ﷻ has mentioned them in glowing terms in His Glorious Book. Notice how many major and minor sins He forgave them, in exchange for an hour—or an instant—of belief. They did nothing but say, from the sincerity of their hearts: *"We believe in the Lord of All the Worlds!"* (26:47). But see how He accepted them and pardoned all their previous sins, and how He made them the chief witnesses [to the Truth] in the Garden of Paradise, for all eternity. Such is the condition of those who acknowledged God ﷻ and affirmed His Oneness for a moment, after all that sorcery, unbelief, error and corruption, so what is the condition of someone who devotes all his life to the affirmation of His Oneness, and sees no one as worthy of that in the two abodes, apart from Him?

Consider the Companions of the Cave [Aṣḥāb al-Kahf], and how they had spent all their lives in the state of unbelief: *When they stood forth and said: "Our Lord is the Lord of the heavens and the earth. We shall cry to no god beside Him"* (18:14). And they took refuge with Him. Notice how He accepted them and pardoned them, then extolled them and honoured them, for He said: *And We turned them over to the right, then over to the left* (18:18).

Notice how He treated them with great respect, and clothed them with awesome dignity, to the point where He said to the noblest of creatures in His sight: *If you had observed them closely, you would surely have turned away from them in flight, and would have been filled with awe of them* (18:18).

Notice, indeed, how He honoured a dog that followed them, to the point of mentioning it several times in His Glorious Book. He assigned it to their custody in this world, and He will cause it to enter the Garden of Paradise in the Hereafter, honoured and revered. Such is His gracious treatment of a dog, which accompanied a group of people who acknowledged Him and affirmed His Oneness for a number of days, without performing any act of worship or service. What does this tell us, then, about His grace in dealing with His believing servant, who has served Him, affirmed His Oneness and worshipped Him for seventy years? What if he lived for seventy thousand years? He would surely be a candidate for servanthood!

Notice how God ﷻ censured Abraham ﷺ for invoking destruction upon the sinners, and how He censured Moses ﷺ in the matter of Qārūn [Korah], for He said: "Qārūn appealed to you for help, but you did not help him. By My Might and Glory, if he asked Me for help, I would help him and pardon him!" Notice how God censured Jonah ﷺ in the matter of his people, for He said: "You feel sorry for a gourd-tree, which I caused to grow for a while, then caused it to wither, but you do not feel sorry for a hundred thousand people or more!" Then notice how He accepted their excuse, and deflected the terrible torment from them, after they had gone astray. Notice how God censured the Chief of the Envoys ﷺ in connection with the following incident: It is related that the Prophet ﷺ entered [the Sanctuary] through the Banī Shaiba Gate, where he saw some people laughing. He said: "Why are you laughing? Let me not see you laughing!" Then, when he was beside the Black Stone [in the Kaʿba], their previous despondency returned to them. He said: "Gabriel came to me and said: 'O Muḥammad, God ﷻ is saying to you: "Why do you make My servants despair of My mercy? *Announce to My servants that I am the All-Forgiving, the All-Compassionate*"''" (15:49).

The Messenger of God ﷺ says: "God ﷻ is More Compassionate with His servant than the tender mother with her child." According to the well-known traditional report, the Prophet ﷺ also said:

> God ﷻ has more than a hundred mercies. He has divided one of them among the jinn, the human race and the animals, so it helps them to feel affection

and sympathy for one another. He has kept ninety-nine of them in store for Himself, so that He may use them to treat His servants mercifully on the Day of Resurrection.

Since God ﷻ has given you a share of one mercy, all of these noble and splendid gifts are available to you, including knowledge of Him, membership in this mercifully blessed Community, and knowledge of the Sunna [the exemplary custom of the Prophet ﷺ], as well as all the other external and internal blessings you enjoy. It is therefore reasonable to hope, from His tremendous grace, that He will perfect all that, for if someone embarks on good work completion is incumbent upon him. It is reasonable to hope that He will grant you an abundant portion from those other ninety-nine mercies. We therefore beseech God ﷻ, invoking His grace and imploring Him not to dash our hopes for His tremendous favour. He is the Generous Master, the Munificent, the All-Compassionate.

§ THIRD ESSENTIAL: WHAT IS TO COME IN THE HEREAFTER

Remembering well what God ﷻ has promised and threatened with regard to the Hereafter. In this connection, we must remember five situations: (1) death, (2) the grave, (3) the Resurrection, (4) the Garden of Paradise, and (5) the Fire of Hell. We must also remember the enormous peril that each of them contains, for the obedient and the disobedient, the negligent and the diligent.

1. As for death, the thought of it reminds me of two men: Ibn Shubruma, who is reported as having said: "Along with ash-Shaʿbī, I paid a visit to an invalid who was lying sick in bed. Another man was by his side, instructing him to say: 'There is no god but God, Alone without any partner [*lā ilāha illa 'llāhu Waḥdah; lā sharīka la-h*],' so ash-Shaʿbī said to the man: 'Be gentle with him!' Then the invalid spoke up, saying: 'Whether you instruct me or do not instruct me, I shall not fail to make that affirmation.' Then he recited: *And He imposed on them the statement of true devotion, for they were worthy of it and deserving of it* (48:26).

"Then ash-Shaʿbī said: 'Praise be to God, who has saved our companion!'"

It is related that a pupil of al-Fuḍail ibn ʿIyās was close to death, so al-Fuḍail entered his presence, sat by his head, and recited the Sūra entitled Yā-Sīn. "O teacher," he said, "do not recite this Sūra." So al-Fuḍail fell silent for a while. Then he instructed him to say: "There is no god but God [*lā ilāha illa 'llāh*]," but the pupil said: "I shall not say it, because I am exempt from it!" He died there and then, so al-Fuḍail went home and spent forty days weeping, without leaving his house.

Then, in a dream, he saw his pupil being dragged towards Hell, so he said: "Why did God deprive you of knowledge and understanding, when you were the most knowledgeable of my pupils?" The pupil replied: "For three reasons: First of all, I was guilty of calumny, for I told my companions the opposite of what I told you. Second, I was guilty of envy. I was envious of my companions. Third, I had a disease, so I went to the physician and asked him about it, and he said: 'You must drink a bottle of wine each year, for, unless you do so, the disease will stay with you.' I acted on his advice."

We take refuge with God ﷻ from His displeasure, which we lack the strength to endure.

I also remember the condition of two other men: ʿAbdu'llāh ibn al-Mubārak (may God bestow His mercy upon him). It is related that when he was close to death, he looked up towards Heaven, laughed, and said: *For the like of this, let the workers work* (37:61). [This Qurʾānic verse reminds me that] I also heard [my Shaikh] Imām al-Ḥaramain ﷺ relate that Professor Abū Bakr (may God bestow His mercy upon him) once said:

I had a companion in the days of teaching. He was a novice devoted to learning, righteous and committed to worshipful service. Despite his dedicated striving, however, he was acquiring only a little knowledge, so we found his condition surprising. Then he fell ill, so he stayed in his place among the saintly friends in the convent [*ribāṭ*], and did not enter the hospital. He continued to exert himself, despite his illness, so his condition deteriorated while I was at his side. While he was like that, he raised his eyes towards Heaven, then said to me: 'O Ibn Fūrak: *For the like of this, let the workers work* (37:61).' He died at that very moment (may God bestow His mercy upon him).

Mālik ibn Dīnār (may God bestow His mercy upon him). It is related that he entered the presence of a neighbour of his, who was close to death. "O Mālik," he said, "two mountains of fire are in front of me, and I am obliged to climb them." Mālik said: "I asked his family about him, and they told me: 'He used to have two measures, one for measuring what he dispensed, and the other for measuring what he received.' I sent for the two measures, and struck one of them against the other till I smashed them both to pieces. Then I asked the man how he was, and he said: 'The matter has only become more serious for me!'"

2. As for the grave and the situation after death, this subject also reminds me of the condition of two men. According to one of the righteous:

I saw Sufyān ath-Thawrī in a dream, after his death, so I asked: "How is your condition, O Abū ʿAbdiʾllāh?" He turned away from me and said: "This is not the time for agnomens." So I rephrased my question and asked: "How is your condition, O Sufyān?" He responded in poetry, saying:

I looked at my Lord directly and He said to me:
"Welcome! Enjoy My good pleasure, O Ibn Saʿīd!
You used to keep vigil when the night turned dark,
with many an ardent tear and a steady heart,
so draw near and choose any palace you wish,
and visit Me, for I am not far away from you."

It is related that someone was seen in a dream, looking very pale, with his hands fettered to his neck. He was asked: "What has God done with you?" so he gave the poetic reply:

Gone is a time with which we used to play,
and this is a time that plays with us.
I am also reminded of the condition of two other men:

It is related that one of the righteous said: "I had a son who was martyred, and I did not see him in a dream until the night when ʿUmar ibn ʿAbd al-ʿAzīz died ﷺ. I saw him that night, so I said: 'O my son, have you not become a corpse?' He said: 'No, but I have been martyred, so I am alive, sustained in the presence of God ﷻ.' I said: 'What has brought you here?' He replied: 'The proclamation was made to the people of Heaven: "Let no Prophet, no champion of Truth, and no martyr stay away from the funeral service of ʿUmar ibn ʿAbd al-ʿAzīz!" I therefore came to attend his funeral service, and now I have come to you, to greet you with the salutation of peace.'"

It is related that Hishām ibn Ḥassān once said: "A young son of mine died, and I saw him in a dream. He appeared as a grey-haired old man, so I said: 'O my son, what is this grey-haired condition?' He replied: 'When so-and-so approached us, Hell emitted a sizzling groan at his approach, so we all turned grey, without exception.'" We take refuge with God, the All-Compassionate, from the painful torment!

3. As for the Resurrection [*Qiyāma*], you must contemplate the saying of God ﷻ: *On the day when We shall muster the truly devout unto the All-Merciful, in fine style, and We shall drive the guilty culprits into Hell, like a herd of beasts* (19:85,86).

One person will emerge from his grave, to find [the heavenly steed] Burāq at its head, as well as the crown and fine garments prepared for him, so he will dress and ride to the Gardens of Bliss. On account of his dignity, he will not be left to walk to the Garden of Paradise on his own two feet. Another will emerge from his grave, to encounter the stokers of Hell [*zabāniya*], along with the shackles and chains that will bind him. They will not let the poor wretch walk to the Fire on his own two feet. He will be dragged to the Inferno on his face. We take refuge with God ﷻ from His displeasure!

I also heard one of the scholars relate that the Prophet ﷺ once said:

> When the Day of Resurrection has arrived, one set of people will emerge from their graves with dromedaries for them to ride. Those dromedaries will have green wings, so they will fly with them over the plains of the Resurrection, until they alight on the walls of the Garden of Paradise. Then, when the angels see them, they will say to one another: "Who are these?" The only response will be: "We do not know. Perhaps they are members of the Community of Muḥammad ﷺ." Then one of the angels will come to them and say: "Who are you?" To which of the communities do you belong?" They will reply: "We belong to the Community of Muḥammad ﷺ," so the angels will say to them: "Have you been subject to the reckoning?" They will say: "No," so the angels will say: "Have you been weighed?" They will again say: "No," so the angels will say: "Have you read your records?" They will again say: "No," so the angels will say: "Go back, for all of that is behind you." They will say: "Have you given us something for which we may be called to account?"

According to another version of this traditional report:

> [They will say to the angels]: "We have not been guilty of anything that would make us deviate or go astray, but we worshipped our Lord until He summoned us, so we have answered Him." A crier will then proclaim [on behalf of the

Lord]: "My servants have told the truth. There is no case to be made against those who do good."

God is All-Forgiving, Compassionate. You have surely heard His saying: *Is he who is hurled into the Fire better, or he who comes secure on the Day of Resurrection?* (41:40).

How splendid is a man who witnesses those terrors, earthquakes, and catastrophes, yet is so secure that no alarm disturbs his heart, and no heaviness weighs it down! We beseech God the Almighty, imploring Him to include you, and us, among His blessed friends. That is not difficult for God (Magnificent is His Majesty)!

4 & 5. As for the Garden of Paradise and the Fire of Hell, you must reflect on the relevant verses [*āyāt*] in the Book of God 🕮. These include His saying: *And their Lord will slake their thirst with a pure drink. [And it will be said unto them]: "Behold, this is a reward for you. Your endeavour has found acceptance"* (76:21, 22).

He has also said, referring to the others [the unbelievers]: [*They will say*]: *"Our Lord, bring us forth out of it! Then, if we revert, we shall be evildoers indeed." He will say: "Slink away into it, and do not speak to Me"* (23:107, 108).

It is also related that they will turn into dogs, barking at one another in the Fire of Hell. We take refuge with God, the Gentle, the All-Compassionate, from the painful torment! According to Yaḥyā ibn Muʿādh ar-Rāzī (may God bestow His mercy upon him):

> We do not know which of the two disasters is more terrible: losing the Gardens of Paradise, or entering the Fires of Hell. As for the Garden, its loss is intolerable. As for the Fire, its torment is insufferable. In any case, however, the loss of the bliss [of Paradise] is easier to bear than the torment of the Inferno. The greatest calamity and the most terrible disaster is the infinite duration [of loss and suffering]. If only the situation had an expiration date, it would at least be easier to contemplate! In fact, however, it will last for all eternity without end, so what heart can bear that prospect? What temperament can endure that with patience? That is why Jesus 🕮 said: "The hearts of the fearful are stopped by remembering the everlasting state of those who are everlastingly doomed."

It was mentioned in the presence of al-Ḥasan [al-Baṣrī] that the last of those who emerge from the Fire will be a man called Hannād. He will have been tormented for a thousand years, while crying: "O Tender One [*Ḥannān*], O

Beneficent One [*Mannān*]!" This made al-Ḥasan weep, and he said: "If only I were Hannād!" His listeners were astonished, so he said: "Woe unto you! Will there not be a day when he comes out [at the end of a thousand years in the Fire]?"

The whole matter, therefore, hinges on one basic point, and that is the point that shatters backs, turns faces pale, make livers dissolve, stops hearts from beating, and causes the servants' eyes to bleed. That is the fear of being deprived of true knowledge [*maʿrifa*], for this is the ultimate fear of the fearful, over which the eyes of the weepers weep. According to one of the righteous: "Anxieties are three in number: (1) Anxiety about worshipful obedience, in that it may not be accepted. (2) Anxiety about sinful disobedience, in that it may not be forgiven. (3) Anxiety about true knowledge, in that it may be stripped away." According to one of the sincerely devout: "In reality, all anxiety is one, and that is anxiety about the deprival of true knowledge. Every other anxiety is insignificant by comparison, since it has a solution."

We are told that Yūsuf ibn Asbāṭ (may God bestow His mercy upon him) once said: "I entered the presence of Sufyān (may God bestow His mercy upon him), who wept throughout every night. I asked him: 'Is this weeping of yours over sins?' He waved a straw, and said: 'Sins are less important to God than this! My only dread is that God may deprive me of Islam."

We beseech God ﷻ, our Beneficent Lord, imploring Him not to try us with an affliction, to grant us much of His bounty, through His gracious favour, and to let us die in the religion of Islam. He is the Most Merciful of the merciful!

We have discussed the cause of the ultimate evil, and its significance, in the book entitled: "Revival of the Religious Sciences [*Iḥyā' ʿUlūm ad-Dīn*]," so you should study it there. The introduction to it here [in the present work] is concise, so try to understand this summary correctly, for the detailed account is more than can be imagined and described. Perhaps you will succeed, with God's help and the blessing of His enabling grace!

You may ask: "Which of the two paths is more practicable, the path of fear or the path of hope?"

The answer will be: Neither by itself, but rather the combination of the two. According to one of the scholars: "If hope prevails over someone, he becomes a Murji'[9] because of it, and he may be in danger of becoming a Khurramī.[10] If fear prevails over someone, he becomes a Ḥarūrī."[11] The point is that the servant should not experience either of the two exclusively, for, in reality, genuine hope is inseparable from genuine fear, and genuine fear is inseparable from genuine hope. That is why, as someone said: "All hope belongs to the people of fear, not of security, and all fear belongs to the people of hope, not of despair."

You may ask: "Is one of the two preferable or more important in any particular situation?"

You should therefore know that if the servant is healthy and strong, fear is more appropriate for him. If he is sick and weak, on the other hand, especially if he is close to the Hereafter, hope is more appropriate. That is what I have heard the scholars say. According to traditional report, God ﷻ says: "I am with those whose hearts are broken from fear of Me."[12]

Hope becomes more appropriate for the servant at that moment [of death], because of his heart being broken, while his fear takes precedence in the time of health, strength and capability. That is why they [whose hearts are broken] are told: *Do not fear and do not grieve!* (41:30).

You may say: "Are there are not many traditional reports concerning the need to think well of God ﷻ, and encouraging that attitude?"

You should therefore know that thinking well of God ﷻ involves being wary of disobeying Him, being afraid of His chastisement, and striving hard in His service.

You should also know that there is a basic principle here, and an important concept, which many people fail to understand correctly. That principle is the difference between hope [*rajā'*] and desire [*umniyya*]. Hope is based on a foundation, whereas desire is not based on a foundation. For instance, if a farmer sows seeds, works hard, and gathers a harvest for threshing, then says: "I hope this will provide me with a hundred *qafīz* [large measures of flour]," that is a valid hope on his part. If another person sows no seeds, and does not work for a single day, but goes off and sleeps for much of the year, then says, when the time of threshing arrives: "I hope I will get a hundred measures of flour out of this," he will be asked: "From where do you get this hope?" That is a desire without foundation.

Likewise in the case of the servant, if he works hard in the service of God ﷻ, refrains from disobedience to God ﷻ, then says: "I hope that God ﷻ will accept this slight effort from me, perfect this shortcoming, magnify this reward, and pardon the mistakes," and if he thinks well [of God], this is a valid hope on his part. On the other hand, if he neglects all that, refrains from acts of worshipful obedience, commits acts of sinful disobedience, and is indifferent to God's displeasure and His approval, to His promise, and His threat, then dares to say: "I hope God ﷻ will grant me the Garden of Paradise and salvation from the Fire of Hell," that is a desire on his part, with no substance to underpin it. He calls it a hope and a good opinion [of God], but that is a mistake and an error on his part. As the poet said:

> You hope for salvation,
>   but you have not followed its courses.
> The ship does not sail on dry land!

This principle is further explained by the saying attributed to the Prophet ﷺ: "The shrewd and skilful person is one who subjugates his lower self, and works for what is after death. The incompetent is one who follows his lower self and his passion, and foists his desires on God ﷻ."

In this context, al-Ḥasan al-Baṣrī ﷺ once said: "Some people are so preoccupied with desires for forgiveness, that they leave this world bankrupt, with no good work to their credit. One of them says: 'I think well of my Lord.' He is lying. If he really thought well of his Lord, he would do good work for His sake." Then al-Ḥasan recited the saying of God ﷻ: *So whoever hopes for the meeting with his Lord, let him do righteous work, and let him give no one any share at all in the worship due unto his Lord* (18:110). [And he recited]: *And that, your thought that you did think about your Lord, has ruined you, and you find yourselves among the lost* (41:23).

According to Jaʿfar aḍ-Ḍabuʿī (may God bestow His mercy upon him): "I saw Abū Maisara, the worshipful servant, and I noticed that his ribs were visible, because he worked so hard. I said: 'May God bestow His mercy upon you! God's mercy is vast indeed!' He was angry at this, and he said: 'Have you seen me show any sign of despair? God's mercy is near to those who do good work!' His words made me weep."

Since all the messengers, all the Abdāl and all the saints were committed, with all this dedicated effort, to worshipful obedience and the avoidance of sinful disobedience, what do you say? Did they not have a good opinion of God ﷻ? Of course they did, for they were very well aware of the vast extent of His mercy, and they had an excellent opinion of His generosity, but they knew that all that, without dedicated effort, was merely desire and delusion. You must therefore consider this important point, reflect on their condition, and wake up from your slumber. God ﷻ is the Custodian of enabling grace!

§ SUMMARY OF THESE ESSENTIALS

The gist of the matter is this: You must remember the vast extent of God's mercy, which has outstripped His wrath and encompassed everything, then remember that you belong to this Community, which is mercifully blessed and noble in the sight of God ﷻ, then remember the abundance of His splendid favour and the perfection of His noble generosity, and that He has addressed His Book to you with the heading: *In the Name of God, the All-Merciful, the All-Compassionate.*

You must also remember the multiplicity of His favours to you, and the blessing He has bestowed upon you, both outwardly and inwardly, without any intercessor or mediator on your behalf.

From another aspect, you must remember the perfection of His majesty and His might, and the magnificence of His authority and His dignity. You must remember the violence of His wrath, which the heavens and the earth cannot withstand. You must remember the enormity of your heedlessness, and the multiplicity of your sins, as well as your coarseness in contrast with the subtlety of His way of working, and the momentousness of His dealing with the all-embracing extent of His knowledge and His awareness of faults [*ʿuyūb*] and mysteries [*ghuyūb*].

Then you must remember the beauty of His promise and His reward, the essence of which no imagination can fathom, as well as the violence of His threat and the agony of His punishment, the recollection of which no heart can bear. Sometimes you must contemplate His gracious favour. Sometimes you must contemplate His torment. Sometimes you must contemplate His kindness and His mercy. Sometimes you must contemplate your lower self, observing its coarse and offensive behaviour.

If you do all this, it will lead you to fear and hope. You will have traveled the central thoroughfare, and avoided the two perilous sides—false security and despair—instead of wandering in them with those who go astray, and perishing with those who perish. You will have drunk the mixed drink of moderation, so you will not perish from the coldness of unadulterated hope, nor from the heat of unadulterated fear. It seems to me that you have reached the goal successfully, and been cured of the two diseases safely. You have found the lower self motivated to practise worshipful obedience, and committed to service by night and by day, without any pause or absent-mindedness, avoiding sinful acts of disobedience and atrocities, so you have finally been relieved of it [as a troublemaker].

As Nawf al-Bikālī said: "When Nawf remembers the Garden of Paradise, his ardent yearning is prolonged, and when he remembers the Fire of Hell, his sleep flies away."

You have now become one of the chosen few, the worshipful elite, whom God ﷻ has described in His saying: *They used to compete with one another in good deeds, and they cried to Us in longing and in fear, and they were submissive unto Us* (21:90).

You have left this dangerous hurdle behind you, with God's consent and the blessing of His enabling grace. You will enjoy so much sweetness and serenity in this world, and so much noble treasure and splendid recompense awaits you in the Hereafter. We beseech God ﷻ to assist you, and us, with the blessing of His enabling grace and His guidance. He is the Most Merciful of the merciful and the Most Generous of the most generous. There is no might nor any power except with God, the All-High, the Almighty.

THE HURDLE OF IMPAIRMENTS

O MY BROTHER, may God support you, and us, with the blessing of His enabling grace! Now that the way is clear to you, and the journey lies straight before you, your next duty is to separate your virtuous endeavour from everything that corrupts it and causes you to lose it. That can only be achieved by the practise of sincere devotion and gratitude, and by avoiding the opposite thereof, for two reasons:

1. The benefit contained in that practise, which is the blessing of acceptance from God ﷻ and the attainment of the reward. Without that acceptance and attainment, you will be rejected and deprived of the reward, in whole or in part. As related in the well-known tradition [ḥadīth], the Prophet ﷺ once said that God ﷻ says: "I am the Most Independent of those who are independent of partnership [shirk]. If a person does a job of work, and makes someone other than Me partner in it, My share belongs to him [the partner], for I accept nothing but that which is purely for Me." Also, it is reported that God ﷻ will say to His servant on the Day of Resurrection, when he seeks the reward for his work: "Were you not given space at the meetings? Were you not the head of the pack in the world? Did you not profit from your buying and selling? Were you not treated with honour?"

§ FIRST IMPAIRMENT: HYPOCRITICAL OSTENTATION

These are examples of the danger and harm [that threaten your endeavour]. As for the danger of hypocritical ostentation [*riyā'*], it involves two ignominies and two disasters.

FIRST, ignominy in secret, in the form of blame in the presence of the angels, as related in the traditional report: "The angels will raise the servant's work aloft, rejoicing in it, but God ﷻ will say: 'Cast him into the Pit [*Sijjīn*], for he did not intend it for My sake!'" That servant and his work will thus be disgraced in the presence of the angels. SECOND, the ignominy of public exposure on the Day of Resurrection, in the presence of all creatures. It is related that the Prophet ﷺ once said:

The ostentatious hypocrite [*murā'ī*] will be addressed on the Day of Resurrection with four names: "O unbeliever [*yā kāfir*], O profligate [*yā fājir*], O traitor [*yā ghādir*], and O loser [*yā khāsir*]! Your endeavour has gone astray, and your recompense has been annulled, so there is no portion for you today. You must seek the recompense from those for whom you used to work, O swindler!"

According to another traditional report: A crier will proclaim on the Day of Resurrection, making all creatures hear: "Where are those who used to serve human beings? Stand up and receive your wages from those for whom you used to work, for I accept no work that anything has adulterated!"

As for the two disasters, they are: FIRST, the loss of the Garden of Paradise. The Prophet ﷺ is reported as having said: "The Garden of Paradise spoke, saying: 'I am unlawful for every miser and ostentatious hypocrite!'" This report conveys two meanings: (1) The miser referred to is someone who is niggardly with the best of speech, that being the declaration: "There is no god but God. Muḥammad is God's Messenger ﷺ." As for the ostentatious hypocrite, he is someone who is guilty of the most flagrant ostentation, for he is the hypocrite who makes a show of his faith [*īmān*] and his affirmation of Divine Oneness [*Tawḥīd*]. This interpretation leaves room for hope [of repentance]. (2) If someone does not desist from niggardliness and ostentation, and does not guard against them, he runs two risks: One is that the wickedness thereof may stick to him, so that he falls into unbelief and forfeits the Garden of Paradise absolutely. The only refuge is with God! The other risk is deprival of faith, which will doom him to the Fire of Hell. We take refuge with God from His displeasure and the violence of His wrath!

The SECOND disaster is entering the Fire of Hell. According to Abū Huraira ‏, the Prophet ‏ once said:

> The first to be summoned on the Day of Resurrection will be [three men]: a man who compiled the Qur'ān, a man who fought in the cause of God, and a man who possessed much wealth.

> God ‏ will say to the Qur'an-reader: "Did I not teach you what I sent down to My Messenger?" He will reply: "Yes indeed, O my Lord!" God will then say: "What action did you take in accordance with what you learned?" To this he will reply: "I acted on it through the watches of the night and the ends of the day." God will say: "You have told a lie," and the angels will say: "You have told a lie." God ‏ will go on to say: "You wished to have people say about you: 'So- and-so is a Qur'ān-reciter,' and that is what they said."

> The owner of wealth will be brought forward, and God ‏ will say: "Did I not bestow abundance upon you, so that I did not leave you in need of anyone?" He will reply: "Yes indeed, O my Lord!" God will then say: "What did you do with what I gave you?" To this he will reply: "I used to provide for my family and make charitable donations." God will say: "You have told a lie," and the angels will say: "You have told a lie." God ‏ will go on to say: "You wished to have people say: 'You are very generous,' and that is what they said."

> The man who was slain in the cause of God will then be brought forward, and God will say: "What did you do?" He will reply: "I was commanded to wage the sacred struggle in Your cause, so I fought until I was killed." God ‏ will say: ""You have told a lie," and the angels will say: "You have told a lie." God will go on to say: "You wished to have people say about you: 'So-and-so is a brave and courageous man,' and that is what they said." God's Messenger ‏ then slapped his hand on his knees, and said: "O Abū Huraira, those will be the first of God's creatures to fuel the Fire of Hell!"

Ibn ʿAbbās ‏ is reported as having said: "I heard God's Messenger ‏ say: 'The Fire of Hell and its inhabitants will scream for refuge from the people guilty of hypocritical display.' "His listeners asked: 'O Messenger of God, how will the Fire of Hell scream for refuge?' He replied: 'With [the noise of] the fierce heat by which they will be tormented.'"

In these ignominies [and disasters] there is an admonition for those endowed with faculties of perception. God ﷻ is the Custodian of guidance, through His gracious favour.

You may say: "Tell me about the real meaning of sincerity [*ikhlāṣ*] and ostentation [*riyā'*], their legal status, and their effect on work."

You must therefore know that sincerity [*ikhlāṣ*], according to our scholars, is twofold: (1) sincerity in work, and (2) sincerity in seeking recompense.

As for sincerity in work, it is the intention to draw near to God ﷻ, to venerate His commandment and to answer His call. The incentive thereto is genuine belief. The opposite of this sincerity is hypocrisy [*nifāq*], which is drawing close to anything other than God ﷻ. According to our own Shaikh (may God bestow His mercy upon him): "Hypocrisy is the corrupt belief held by the hyprocrite [*munāfiq*] about God ﷻ."

As for sincerity in seeking recompense, it is the intention to obtain the benefit of the Hereafter by doing good work. Our own Shaikh (may God bestow His mercy upon him) used to say: "It is the intention to obtain the benefit of the Hereafter by means of something irrefutably good, the best that the servant can possibly do, inasmuch as it is done in the hope of obtaining that benefit."

The Disciples [*Ḥawāriyyūn*] said to Mary's son Jesus ﷺ: "Who is sincere in his actions?" He replied: "Someone who works for the sake of God, without needing to have anyone praise him for his work." This is an allusion to abstinence from ostentation, and he mentioned it specifically because ostentation is the strongest of all the causes that confound sincerity.

According to al-Junaid: "Sincerity is the purification of deeds from pollutants." According to al-Fuḍail: "Sincerity is constant vigilance and forgetting all worldly pleasures." This is the perfect explanation. Sayings about this subject are numerous, but there is no point in quoting many more, now that the true facts have been disclosed.

When the [Prophet] ﷺ—Chief of the first and the last—was asked about sincerity, he said: "You say: 'My Lord is God,' then you act correctly, as you have been commanded. In other words: "You must not serve your passion and your lower self. You must serve none but your Lord, and act correctly in His worshipful service, as you have been commanded." This is an instruction to put everything apart from God ﷻ completely outside the scope of consideration. That is sincerity in the true sense.

The opposite of sincerity is ostentation, which is the intention to acquire the benefit of this world by doing the work of the Hereafter. There are two kinds of ostentation: (1) unmitigated ostentation and (2) mitigated ostentation. In its unmitigated form, what you intend by it is to gain the benefit of this world, and nothing else. In its mitigated form, it means that you intend to combine both the benefit of this world and the benefit of the Hereafter.

Such is the definition of the two [sincerity and ostentation]. As for their effect, sincerity in work causes you to perform the work as a virtuous deed [*qurba*], while sincerity in seeking recompense causes you to make it worthy of acceptance, abundant recompense and great respect. Hypocrisy [*nifāq*] invalidates the work, and prevents it from being a virtuous deed, worthy of the reward described in God's promise.

Unmitigated ostentation does not arise from one who knows the Truth, according to some of the scholars, and if it did, it would cancel half of the reward. Others maintain that unmitigated ostentation does sometimes arise from one who knows the Truth, and that it takes away half of the portions [of the reward], while mitigated ostentation takes away a quarter of the portions. The correct opinion, according to our own Shaikh (may God bestow His mercy upon him), is that unmitigated ostentation does not arise from one who knows the Truth, so long as he remembers the Hereafter, but only during absent-mindedness. According to the preferred opinion, the effect of ostentation is the withholding of acceptance and reduction in the reward, though it [the reduction] cannot be quantified as one half or one quarter.

The full explanation of these questions is a very lengthy matter, and we have discussed them exhaustively in the book entitled: *Revival of the Religious Sciences* [*Iḥyā' 'Ulūm ad-Dīn*]. We have also provided extensive treatment of the subject in *Secrets of Religious Practises* [*Asrār Muʿāmalāt ad-Dīn*].

You may ask: "Where is sincerity appropriate, and in which acts of worshipful obedience is it necessary?"

You must therefore know that actions, according to some of the scholars, are divided into three parts: (1) One part involves the two kinds of sincerity in combination, and that is essential outer worship [like the ritual prayer]. (2) One part involves nothing of either, and that is essential inner worship [like faith and trust]. (3) One part involves sincerity in seeking recompense, without sincerity in work, and that is the use of permissible concessions in preparation [for worshipful service]. According to our own Shaikh (may God bestow His mercy upon him): "Sincerity in work is involved in every action, among the essential acts of worship, that may conceivably deviate towards anything other than God ﷻ, so most of the internal acts of worship involve sincerity in work."

As for sincerity in seeking recompense, according to the shaikhs of the Karramiyya sect: "It is not involved in the internal acts of worship, since no one witnesses them except God ﷻ, so the motives of ostentation are precluded from them. Sincerity in seeking recompense is therefore unnecessary." Our own Shaikh (may God bestow His mercy upon him) used to say: "If the servant who is drawn close to God ﷻ performs internal acts of worship, but does so with the intention of obtaining the benefit of this world, that is also a form of ostentation."

In my own opinion, it is not unlikely, therefore, that the two kinds of sincerity are involved in many of the internal acts of worship. By the same token, the two kinds of sincerity are also necessary, in combination, when supererogatory acts of worship are undertaken. As for the use of permissible concessions in preparation [for worshipful service], this involves sincerity in seeking recompense, but not sincerity in work, since these concessions are not adequate in themselves to constitute virtuous conduct, but only as a means of preparation for such conduct.

You may say: "So much for where the two kinds of sincerity are appropriate. Now explain their timing in relation to the action."

You should therefore know that sincerity in work must accompany the action, without a doubt, and it may not be postponed till later. As for sincerity in seeking recompense, it may be postponed until after the action. According to some of the scholars: "The significant point is the time when the work has been concluded. Once the servant has finished his work, in a state of sincerity or ostentation, the matter is settled and he cannot go back and change it." According to the shaikhs of the Karrāmiyya sect: "So long as the servant has not obtained the benefit sought by means of ostentation, it is possible for him to apply sincerity to his work, but if he has obtained that benefit, the opportunity is lost."

According to one of the scholars: "In the case of an obligatory religious duty [*farīḍa*], the possibility of applying sincerity to it lasts until death. As for supererogatory devotions [*nawāfil*], there is no such possibility, The difference between them is that God ﷻ has imposed the obligatory religious duty on the servant, so His gracious favour and facilitation are hoped for in its performance. As for the supererogatory duty, the servant has imposed it on himself, and made it his own responsibility, so he is accountable in accordance with the responsibility he has assumed."

There is a useful lesson in this discussion of the subject. That is to say, if someone has been guilty of ostentation in an act of work, or of omitting sincerity, it is possible for him to amend that situation and correct it, in one of the ways we have previously described. In reporting the doctrines of the scholars in such detail, our purpose is based on our knowledge of the present scarcity of active practitioners [of good work], and the lack of interest in the pursuit of this path. Our purpose is also to assist the novice in worshipful service, for if he does not find a cure for his illness in one opinion, he will find it in another, due to the diversity of diseases and symptoms, the defects of actions and their dire consequences. You must understand correctly, if God ﷻ so wills.

You may ask: "Does every act of work need a separate affirmation of sincerity?"

You should therefore know that the scholars have differed about that. Some maintain that every act of work needs a separate affirmation of sincerity. Others maintain the permissibility of a single affirmation of sincerity for a number of acts of worship. As for those acts of which the basic elements are prescribed, like the ritual prayer [*ṣalāt*] and ablution [*wuḍū'*], a single affirmation of sincerity is sufficient, because one of them is linked to another in rightness or wrongness, so they are like a single item.

You may ask: "If the servant performs his good work with the intention of obtaining a worldly favour from God ﷻ, and not with the intention of gaining anything from people, such as praise or fame or benefit, does that constitute ostentation?"

You should recognise that as unmitigated ostentation. According to our scholars (may God bestow His mercy upon them): "The crucial factor in ostentation is the intended object, regardless of whom you intend to impress. If a worldly favour is your intended object in performing good work, that amounts to ostentation, whether you seek to obtain the favour from God ﷻ or from people." God ﷻ has said: *If someone desires the harvest of the Hereafter, We shall give him an increase in his harvest, and whoever desires the harvest of this world, We shall give him some of it, but in the Hereafter he will have no share* (42:20).

You may ask: "What if the worldly benefit sought from God ﷻ is sympathy from people and preparation for God's service? Is that a case of ostentation?"

You must therefore know that sympathy does not consist of material wealth, prestige, and worldly vanities. It consists of contentment and reliance on the sufficient provision of God ﷻ.

As for preparation for the worshipful service of God ﷻ, if that is the servant's intended object, it is not a case of ostentation. That preparation is connected with the business of the Hereafter and its means of attainment, and that becomes his purpose, absolutely. If this kind of object is intended by the performance of good work, the intention does not constitute a form of ostentation. That is because these matters become good by virtue of that intention, or come to be classed as deeds of the Hereafter, and the intention to do good work is not a form of ostentation.

The same is true if your intention is to gain respect in the sight of the general public, or affectionate regard from the shaikhs and the imāms, provided that your purpose therein is to be in a position to support the doctrine [*madhhab*] of the upholders of the Truth, or to refute the advocates of heretical innovations, or to disseminate knowledge, or to urge people to engage in worshipful service. Your purpose must be along these lines, not to gain personal honour for its own sake, nor to promote your worldly interest. All of this constitutes rightly guided aspiration and praiseworthy intentions, so no part of it comes under the heading of ostentation, since the purpose of it is, in reality, the business of the Hereafter.

You should also know that I asked one of our shaikhs about the custom of our saints, regarding the recitation of the Sūra of the Event [*al-Wāqiʿa*] on the days of hardship. I said: "Surely the intended purpose is that God ﷻ may dispel that hardship from them, and grant them some worldly bounty, in keeping with the normal state of affairs. So how can it be correct to seek the bounty of this world, in exchange for the work of the Hereafter?"

In his reply, the Shaikh (may God bestow His mercy upon him) said, in effect: "Their intended purpose is that God ﷻ may supply them with sufficient sustenance, or basic nourishment, to prepare them for the worshipful service of God ﷻ, and to give them strength for the study of knowledge. Such intentions are good, not worldly."

You should also know that this customary practise, meaning the recitation of this Sūra in time of hardship, for the sake of sustenance and the satisfaction of need, has been transmitted in reports concerning the Prophet ﷺ and the Companions ﷺ. For instance, when Abū Maʿsūd was blamed for leaving his children with nothing from this world, he said: "I have left them the Sūra of the Event [al-Wāqiʿa]!" From that root in the Sunna, this custom has branched into the practises of our scholars (may God bestow His mercy upon them). Had it not [been rooted in the Sunna], they would not have recognised the value of praising God ﷻ for hardship in this world, or for comfort therein.

As it is, our scholars take full advantage of the narrowness and hardship of this world, and vie with one another in the process. They count it as a tremendous favour from God ﷻ. On the other hand, if they see a worldly benefit coming to them from God ﷻ, something that most people would simply regard as a gracious gift and blessing, they are afraid that it may be a temptation from God ﷻ and an affliction. That is because they are happily accustomed to traveling and going hungry in most situations, and their leaders say: "Hunger is the capital of our wealth!"

This is the basic doctrine of the masters of Sufism, and it is my doctrine and the doctrine of my shaikhs. That was also the guiding principle of our righteous forebears. As for the shortcoming of some more recent types, it is unworthy of consideration. We mention this distinction only to spare them [our righteous forebears] from being blamed by a critical outsider, ignorant of the goals of the people [of the Spiritual Path], or in case a sound-hearted novice misunderstands them and fails to learn the truth.

You may ask: "How can this [recitation of the Sūra in times of hardship] be consistent with the state of the people of knowledge, exclusive dedication [to worship] and abstinence, and the masters of patience and spiritual training?"

You should therefore know that this practise is taken from the Sunna [of the Prophet ﷺ]. Furthermore, the goal is the attainment of contentment and preparation [for worshipful service], not the pursuit of greed, carnal desire, and weakness in the face of difficulty and hardship. Most of what you see in the wake of that [recitation of the Sūra] is contentment of the heart [*qalb*], loss of the dog [*kalb*] of hunger, and detachment from the gluttonous appetite for food. That is known by those who put it to the test of experience. You must understand all this successfully, if God ﷻ so wills.

§ SECOND IMPAIRMENT: VAIN CONCEIT

The avoidance of vain conceit ['*ujb*] is incumbent upon you for two reasons: FIRST, it presents a barrier to enabling grace and assistance from God ﷻ, so he who is vainly conceited is left in the lurch. If the servant is cut off from enabling grace and assistance from God ﷻ, he perishes so quickly! That is why the Prophet ﷺ once said: "There are three causes of perdition: a greed obeyed, a passion pursued, and a man's vain conceit in himself."

SECOND, it corrupts righteous work. That is why the Messiah ﷺ once said: "O company of the Disciples, how many a lamp has been blown out by the wind, and how many a worshipful servant has been corrupted by vain conceit!" Worshipful service is the purpose and the benefit [of righteous work], and this vice deprives the servant so that he obtains nothing good. Even if he does obtain something good, a little of that [vain conceit] is enough to corrupt it, so he is left with nothing at all. He is therefore obliged to be on his guard against that, and to exercise great caution. God is the Custodian of enabling grace and protection!

You may ask: "So what is the real meaning of vain conceit? What is its significance, its effect and its legal status? Explain that to us!"

You must therefore know that the real meaning of vain conceit is the aggrandizement of righteous work. As defined in detail by our scholars (may God bestow His mercy upon them), it is the servant's attribution of the honour obtained by righteous work to something other than God ﷻ, or to people, or to the lower self. They have said: "Vain conceit may be threefold, inasmuch as it may be attributed to all of these three together: the lower self, fellow creatures, and the thing [that is other than God]. It may also be twofold, inasmuch as it

86

may be attributed to two of these, or singlefold, inasmuch as it may be attributed to only one of them."

The opposite of vain conceit is gratitude, which means remembering that it [the honour obtained by righteous work] is due to the enabling grace of God ﷻ, and that He is the One who has honoured the servant and magnified his reward and his worth. This remembrance is an obligatory duty in the presence of the causes of vain conceit, and a supererogatory duty at other times.

As for the effect of vain conceit on the servant's work, one of our scholars has said: "If someone is vainly conceited, he is waiting for annulment [*iḥbāṭ*]. If he repents before his death, he will be safe; otherwise he will suffer annulment." This opinion was also held by Muḥammad ibn Ṣābir, one of the shaikhs of the Karrāmiyya sect. According to him, annulment means that the servant's work is stripped of all good names, so that he is entitled to no reward and no praise, none whatsoever. According to another, *iḥbāṭ* means removal of the multiplication [of the reward], and nothing else.

You may ask: "For the servant who knows the Truth, how can there be any doubt that God ﷻ is the One who has enabled his righteous work, magnified his worth and multiplied his reward, through His grace and favour?"

You must therefore know that here we have a subtle hint and a noble treasure, indicating that, when it comes to vain conceit, people are of three types:

1. Those who are vainly conceited in every situation. They are [the sects known as] the Muʿtazila[13] and the Qadariyya,[14] who do not believe that God ﷻ grants them any favour in their actions, and who disavow His special help and enabling grace. That is because of a doubt that has prevailed upon them.

2. Those who gratefully acknowledge their indebtedness to God ﷻ in every situation. They are the rightly guided, who are not vainly conceited about any of their works. That is because they have been endowed with a perceptive faculty of understanding, and singled out for special assistance.

3. The mixers, who constitute the majority of the people of the Sunna. They sometimes come to their senses, so they gratefully acknowledge God's favour. Sometimes they are heedless, so they become vainly conceited in that regard, due to the influence of heedlessness, the gap in earnest endeavour, and the deficiency in perceptive understanding.

You may ask: "What is the state of the Qadariyya and the Mu'tazila with regard to their actions?"

You must therefore know that there are differences of opinion about that. Some say that their work is annulled on account of their belief. Others say: "In general, work is not annulled on account of a belief held by one the sects of Islam, unless every act of work is specifically viewed with vain conceit, just as the belief of the people of the Sunna does not automatically prevent vain conceit about every act of work, unless it is specifically accompanied by grateful acknowledgement [of God's favour]."

§ OTHER IMPAIRMENTS

Someone may ask: "Apart from vain conceit and ostentation, is work threatened by there any other impairment [*qādiḥ*]?"

The answer will be: "Yes indeed, those two are not the only impairments, but we have singled them out because they are the central point, around which many related topics revolve." According to one of the shaikhs: "In his work, the servant has a duty to guard against ten things: (1) hypocrisy [*nifāq*] (2) ostentation [*riyā'*], (3) mixing, (4) boasting, (5) harm, (6) regret, (7) vain conceit, (8) sorrow, (9) disdain, and (10) fear of people's criticism."

As our own Shaikh (may God bestow His mercy upon him) has mentioned, each of these ten must be actively countered by its opposite: (1) The opposite of hypocrisy [*nifāq*] is sincerity [*ikhlāṣ*] in work. (2) The opposite of ostentation [*riyā'*] is sincerity in seeking recompense. (3) The opposite of mixing is singular devotion. (4) The opposite of boasting is submitting the work to God ﷻ. (5) The opposite of harm is keeping the work safe. (6) The opposite of regret is commitment of the lower self [to good work]. (7) The opposite of vain conceit is grateful acknowledgement [of God's favour]. (8) The opposite of sorrow is taking full advantage of the benefit. (9) The opposite of disdain is respectful recognition of the enabling grace [of God]. (10) The opposite of fear of people's criticism is the dread [of offending God].

You should also know that hypocrisy [*nifāq*] annuls the work, that ostentation [*riyā'*] causes its rejection, and that boasting and harm annul [the reward of] charitable giving absolutely and immediately. According to some of the shaikhs (may God bestow His mercy upon him), they only annul its multiplications.

As for regret, it annuls the work, according to all the scholars, while vain conceit removes the multiplications of [the reward of] the work, and sorrow, disdain and fear of criticism diminish the gravity [*razāna*] of the work.

This means that acceptance and rejection, in the view of those who seek knowledge, depend on various kinds of respect and belittlement, and annulment is the cancellation of benefits acquired by the deed. Annulment sometimes takes the form of cancellation of the reward itself, and sometimes of cancellation of its multiplication. The reward is a benefit determined by the deed itself, as well as its contextual value and significance, while its multiplication is an addition to this. The gravity [*razāna*] of the work is also an addition, resulting from other associated factors, such as benefit provided to one of the people of goodness, then to parents, then to one of the prophets. There may be instances where gravity is added, but there is no multiplication [of the reward].

This is an exposition of what I have ascertained about these concepts, so try to understand that. God ﷻ is the source of enabling grace!

You must surmount this perilous hurdle in the utmost state of wariness, for it is fraught with hazardous intersections and stretches of desert. The owner of the merchandise of acts of worshipful obedience has surmounted all those previous hurdles, and endured all those hardships, and he has thus amassed a noble and splendid store of worshipful service. He is not afraid for that merchandise of his, except on this hurdle, for it contains hazardous intersections where he risks being robbed of his merchandise, and stretches of desert where evils may lurk, threatening to corrupt his worshipful obedience. The most dangerous of all these perils, and those most likely to strike, are these two highway robbers: ostentation [*riyā'*] and vain conceit [*'ujb*]. Let us therefore describe each one of them in sufficient detail, so that you may recognise their essential features, with God's consent and if God ﷻ so wills.

As for ostentation, you must observe these four essentials:

FIRST ESSENTIAL of all, you must remember the saying of God ﷻ: *It is God who has created seven heavens, and of the earth their like. The Command comes down between them gradually, so that you may know that God is Powerful over all things, and that God has encompassed everything in knowledge* (65:12).

It is as if God ﷻ is saying: "I have created the heavens and the earth and all that is between them, in the form of all these works and wonders of creation, and I have paid you enough attention for you to realise that I am All-Powerful, All-Knowing. In spite of all that, you perform two cycles of ritual prayer [rak'atain] with so many faults and shortcomings, and you attach so little importance to My watching over you, My knowledge of you, My commendation of you and My appreciation of you, that you love to have your fellow creatures praise you for that [performance of ritual prayer]. Is that a sign of loyalty? Is that a sign of intelligence, the kind of intelligence that anyone would be pleased to possess? Woe unto you, for you surely do not comprehend!"

THE SECOND ESSENTIAL is this: Suppose that someone had a precious jewel, for which he could have set the price at a million gold coins, yet he sold it for a penny. Would that not be a tremendous loss, an atrocious stupidity, and a clear sign of low ambition, lack of knowledge, weakness of vision and feebleness of intellect? As for what the servant gains by his work, in the form of praise and worldly vanities from his fellow creatures, in relation to the good pleasure of the Lord of All the Worlds, His appreciation, His commendation and His reward, it is less than a penny beside a million gold coins, and many times that, or even beside this whole world, and even more and greater still. It is surely part of the manifest loss [al-khusrān al-mubīn], that you should forfeit those noble and glorious blessings in exchange for these despicable worldly things!

In order to escape from this low ambition, you must aim for the Hereafter and let this world follow after you. Better still, you must seek the Lord, and Him Alone, for He will grant you the two abodes, since He is the Owner of them both. As He has said: *Whoever desires the reward of this world, with God is the reward of this world and the Hereafter* (4:134).

The Prophet ﷺ once said: "God ﷻ will surely grant this world in exchange for the work of the Hereafter, but He will not grant the Hereafter in exchange for the work of this world."

If you are sincere in your intention, and your ambition is solely for the Hereafter, you will therefore gain the Hereafter and this world together. If you seek this world, the Hereafter will immediately depart from you, and you may not obtain what you seek in this world. Even if you do obtain it, you will not keep it for long, so you will soon have lost both this world and the Hereafter. You must therefore consider this with care, O intelligent one!

THE THIRD ESSENTIAL is this: If the creature for whose sake you work, and whose approval you seek, knew that you were working for his sake, he would hate you, despise you, scorn you and belittle you. So how can the intelligent man work for the sake of someone who, if he knew that he was seeking his approval, would despise him and scorn him? You must therefore work, O miserable wretch, for the sake of the One who, if you work for His sake, make Him the goal of your effort, and seek His approval thereby, will love you, give to you and honour you, until He is well pleased with you, makes you independent of everything, and satisfies you completely. You must understand this well, if you are intelligent.

THE FOURTH ESSENTIAL is this: If someone is capable of the effort that will earn him the approval of the mightiest king in this world, but he uses that effort to seek the approval of a wretched street sweeper, that will be a sign of foolishness and stupidity on his part, and it will bring misfortune upon him. He will be asked: "Why do you need the approval of this street sweeper, when it is possible for you to win the approval of the king? Suppose the street sweeper is displeased with you, because of the king's displeasure? You will then lose everything!" This is the condition of the ostentatious hyprocrite.

Why do you need to please a weak and despicable creature, when you are capable of obtaining the good pleasure of God, the Lord of All the Worlds, the All-Sufficing? If your aspiration has been feeble, and your perception blurred, such that you have inevitably sought the approval of a creature, your way out is to dedicate your intention and devote your effort solely to God ﷻ. The hearts and the forelocks [of His creatures] are in His hand, so He will incline their hearts towards you, attach their feelings to you, and fill their breasts with love for you. From that you will gain what you cannot gain by your exertion and your endeavour. If you do not follow this advice, but work with the intention of pleasing creatures, instead of God ﷻ, He will turn hearts away from you, cause feelings to recoil from you, and make creatures displeased with you. You will thus obtain the displeasure of God ﷻ and the displeasure of creatures combined. What a dreadful loss and deprivation!

According to al-Ḥasan [al-Baṣrī]: "A man used to say: 'By God, I shall worship God with a worship for which I shall be remembered!' He was always the first to enter the mosque, and the last to leave it. No one ever saw him, unless he was praying at the time of prayer, fasting without breaking fast, or sitting in the circle of remembrance [dhikr]. He kept that up for seven months, so he never passed by a group of people without their saying: 'May God deal with this ostentatious hypocrite!' He therefore reproached his lower self, telling it: 'I see that I am getting nowhere. Let me devote all my work to God!' He added nothing to the work he had been doing before that except that his intention changed for the better. From then on, whenever he passed by people, they would say: 'God has bestowed His mercy on so-and-so. He has now moved in the right direction.'" Then al-Ḥasan recited the Qur'ānic verse: *As for those who believe and do righteous deeds, the All-Merciful will surely grant them love* (19:96). The poet spoke the truth when he said:

> O you who desire praise and reward
> for a deed, your desire is to no avail.
> God has thwarted the ostentatious hypocrite,
> and annulled the effort and the labour.
> If someone hopes to meet a Lord,
> he must act sincerely from fear of offending Him.
> Eternal life and the Fire are in His hands,
> so show Him [your deeds] and He will give you the benefit.
> People have nothing in their possession,
> so why do you show them an error?

As for vain conceit ['ujb], let us mention the following essential points:

FIRST ESSENTIAL: No real value accrues to the servant's work, except through the approval and acceptance conferred by God. Otherwise, you see the hired workman toiling all day for a couple of dirhams [silver coins], and the watchman staying awake all night for a couple of *dāniqs* [each worth one sixth of a dirham]. The same applies to craftsmen and professionals, each of whom works by night and day, so the value of that work is a number of silver coins. If you dedicate your work to God ﷻ, and spend one day fasting for the sake of God ﷻ, your fasting on that day will be priceless, if He is well pleased with it and accepts it. God ﷻ has said: *Surely those who endure with patience will be paid their wages in full without reckoning* (39:10).

According to the traditional report, [the Prophet 🕊 once said], that [God says]: "I have prepared for My fasting servants that which no eye has ever seen, of which no ear has ever heard, and which has never occurred to the heart of a human being."

Well, this day of yours, the material value of which is a couple of silver coins, along with the toil and trouble you endure, has acquired all this spiritual value through the postponement of breakfast till the evening! If you spent the night in vigil for the sake of God 🕊, and devoted it sincerely to Him, your vigil would be priceless in nobility and preciousness. God 🕊 has said: *So no soul knows what comfort is kept secretly in store for them, as a reward for what they used to do* (32:17).

This night of yours, the material value of which is a couple of *dāniqs* or two dirhams, would thus acquire all this spiritual worth and value. Indeed, [you would obtain this enormous benefit] if you devoted a short time to God, and performed two light cycles of ritual prayer in that time, or even a single breath, in which you said: "There is no god but God [*lā ilāha illa 'llāh*]!" God 🕊 has said: *And whoever does right, whether male or female, and is a believer, such will enter the Garden, where they will be nourished without stint* (40:40).

This is one of those breaths of yours that have no value in the sight of the people of this world, nor in your own sight, so how many like it do you waste for nothing, and how much time passes by you with no benefit? Yet that breath could acquire this tremendous worth, if it happened to be pleasing to God 🕊, for He would magnify its worth, and its value would be multiplied by His gracious favour.

It is therefore incumbent on the intelligent person to recognise the insignificance of his work, and the paucity of its worth as such. He must acknowledge only the gracious favour of God 🕊, which He has conferred upon him by ennobling the value of his work and magnifying its reward. He must beware of acting in a way that is not appropriate for God 🕊, and that does not gain His approval, so that his work loses the value it has acquired, and reverts to its trivial price in dirhams or *dāniqs*, or even less than that.

For the sake of comparison, consider the case of a bunch of grapes or a sheaf of sweet basil, the market value of which is a *dāniq*. If someone presents it to a king, in spite of its triviality, and it meets with approval, the king may give him a thousand gold coins for it, on account of the good pleasure it has evoked. Something priced at a pip has thus become worth a thousand gold coins. If the king is not pleased with it, however, and hands it back to him, it reverts to its trifling value of a pip or a *dāniq*. The same applies to the case that interests us, so wake up, recognise the gracious favour of God ﷻ, and preserve your work from that which mars it in the sight of God ﷻ!

THE SECOND ESSENTIAL point is this: As you know, the king in this world provides someone with rations, in the form of food, or drink, or clothes, or a few gold or silver coins that are soon spent. In exchange, that person serves him through the watches of the night and the day, with all the abasement and humiliation that entails. He stands before the king until his legs turn numb, and he runs in front of him when he goes riding. He sometimes needs to be on guard at his door throughout the night. An enemy may appear, so he will need to fight the foe, sacrificing his irreplaceable spirit for the king's sake. He endures all this service, inconvenience, danger and harm, for the sake of that pitiful and trifling benefit, although it is really from God ﷻ, and the king is merely in the position of an instrument. It is your Lord who created you, when you were nothing. Then He brought you up and trained you well. Then He blessed you with outer and inner blessings in your religion, your person and your worldly life, to an extent unfathomable by your understanding and your imagination. He said (More Glorious is He than any other sayer): *And if you try to reckon the bounty of God, you will never count it. The human being is indeed a wrongdoer, an ingrate* (14:34).

You perform two cycles of ritual prayer, with all the faults and vices you include in them, and knowing what He has promised for them in the future, in the form of excellent reward and various gifts of grace, so you should treat that [performance of prayer] with great respect, yet you are vainly conceited about it. That is not the mark of an intelligent person, if you take notice!

THE THIRD ESSENTIAL point is this: The king is the one who is served by the governors and the commanders, the one before whom the leaders and the dignitaries stand at attention, whose service is conducted by the clever and the wise, whose praise is sought by the intelligent and the scholars, and in front of whom walk the elders and the chiefs. Suppose the king permits a plebeian or a villager to enter his door, as an act of kindness and care for him, so that he rubs shoulders with those governors, leaders and elders, and with those who are distinguished in his service and his commendation, and suppose he assigns him a known station in his presence, and views his acts of service with the eye of approval, even though they are flawed and faulty. People will surely say about that commoner: "This miserable wretch has received great favour and splendid attention from the king!" Then, if this miserable wretch expects the king to show gratitude for that faulty service, if he takes great pride in it, and is vainly conceited about it, people will surely say: "That is a very stupid fool, or a lunatic, who understands nothing at all!"

Once this point has been established, we may go on to say that our God [*Ilāh*] is the King who is glorified by the seven heavens and the earth, and by all that they contain. There is nothing that does not glorify His praise. He who is Worthy of worship is the One to whom those in the heavens and on earth bow down in prostration, willingly or unwillingly. The servants at His door include Gabriel the Trustworthy, Michael, Isrāfīl and 'Izrā'īl, the Bearers of the Heavenly Throne, the Cherubs and the Spiritual Beings, and all the Angels Brought Near, whose number is counted only by God, the Lord of All the Worlds. They are present in their lofty stations, in their visible forms, and in their splendid acts of worshipful service.

The following are also included among those who are servants at His door: Adam, Noah, Abraham, Moses, Jesus and Muḥammad, the best of all creatures, as well as all the other prophets and messengers ﷺ, in their exalted degrees, their honourable and glorious virtues, their noble stations, and their majestic and splendid customs.

Then come the scholars, the religious leaders, the righteous and the ascetics, in their magnificent degrees, their clean and pure bodies, and their many sincere and manifest acts of worshipful service.

The lowliest of the servants at His door are the kings and tyrants of this world, who prostrate themselves humbly before him with their chins on the ground, rub their faces in the dust, and present their needs to Him, weeping, wailing and moaning. They acknowledge their servitude to Him, and confess their own deficiency, bowing down in humble prostration, so He sometimes casts a glance at them and fulfils a need for them, by His gracious favour, or pardons a mistake for them, by His noble generosity.

Regardless of this Might, Majesty, Sovereignty and Perfection of His, God has granted you permission [to enter His service] in spite of your wretchedness, your faults and your impurities. You are the kind of person who might not receive permission from the chief of your town, if you applied to him for permission. If you speak to the governor of your district, he may not speak to you. If you bow down to the ground before the ruler of your country, he may not pay attention to you. Nevertheless, God (Magnificent is His Majesty) has granted you permission to worship Him, to extol Him, and to address Him in speech. You may even direct a request to Him, and express it to Him frankly, asking Him to fulfil your need and satisfy your concerns. He will be pleased with your two cycles of ritual prayer, with all their faults. Indeed, He will prepare for you a reward that would never occur to the human heart, yet you are vainly conceited about these two cycles of ritual prayer! You think you have done a great deal of work, and you are very proud of your performance. You do not acknowledge the gracious favour that God has bestowed upon you. What a bad servant you are, and what an ignorant person!

God is the One from whom we seek help. To Him we complain of this ignorant lower self, and in Him we put all our trust.

Let us now consider the following scenario: The mighty king grants permission for gifts to be presented to him, so into his presence come the commanders, the elders, the chiefs, the noblemen and the rich, bearing all kinds of gifts, such as valuable jewels, precious treasures and magnificent properties. Then a greengrocer comes with a bunch of vegetables, or a villager brings a basket of grapes, equal in value to a *dāniq* or a pip, so he enters the king's presence and rubs shoulders with those elders and rich men, with their many noble gifts. The king accepts that poor man's gift with obvious approval and good pleasure, and awards him a precious cloak of honour. That surely represents the utmost favour and noble generosity on the king's part!

Suppose this poor man expects the king to grovel in gratitude for his gift. Suppose he is vainly conceited about it, takes great pride in it, and forgets to acknowledge the king's gracious favour. People will surely say: "This is a lunatic, mentally deranged, or a stupid fool with bad manners, extremely ignorant!"

What is now required of you, therefore, when you keep vigil at night for the sake of God, and perform two cycles of ritual prayer for His sake? It is that you must think of the many servants who are keeping vigil this night for the sake of God 🕌, in all the regions of the earth, on land and at sea, on the mountains and in the towns, from the ranks of the rightly guided, the champions of Truth, the fearful, the ardent, the dedicated and the humbly submissive. You must consider how much is being presented at this very moment, at the door of God 🕌, in the form of pure worship and genuine service, performed in fear of offending Him, with clean tongues, weeping eyes, devout hearts, immaculate breasts and unstained limbs.

As for your ritual prayers, even if you have spared no effort in refining them and observing their rules, and in performing them with sincerity, they will hardly be suitable for the presence of this Almighty King. They will hardly compare with those acts of worship that are being offered there [at the door of God 🕌]. How can they compare, when you have acted with a negligent heart, mixed with all kinds of faults, a body defiled by the filth of sins, and a tongue stained by all kinds of disobedience and transgression? How can this be fit to be conveyed into that presence? How can it be worthy of being offered to the Lord of Might and Glory?

Our Shaikh (may God bestow His mercy upon him) once said: "Look hard, O intelligent one! Have you ever directed one of your ritual prayers towards Heaven, like a table of food that you sent to the homes of the rich?" Abū Bakr al-Warrāq used to say: "I have never concluded a ritual prayer without feeling ashamed of it. My sense of shame was always greater than that felt by a woman after unlawful sexual intercourse!"

The Noble and Generous Lord 🕌 has magnified the worth of these two cycles of ritual prayer, by His sheer generosity and gracious favour, and He has promised for them the abundant reward that He has promised. You are His servant and you are in His employ. You have done what you have done through His enabling grace and His facilitation. In spite of all that, however, you are vainly conceited about your work, and you forget God's gracious favour. This, by God, is utterly astonishing! The like of it could hardly emanate from anyone but a thoughtless ignoramus, a mindlessly negligent person, or a dead and empty heart. We beseech God 🕌 to grant us sufficient provision, through His grace and favour!

THE PATH OF THE WORSHIPFUL SERVANTS

§ SUBTLETIES OF THESE IMPAIRMENTS

After all that has been said above, you must wake up from your slumber, O man, on this hurdle! If not, you will be among the losers, for this is the toughest, hardest, harshest and most bruising hurdle that has confronted you on this path. It is the culmination of all the previous hurdles, so, if you surmount it safely, you will gain great benefit and profit. If the opposite is the case, all effort has been to no avail, hope has been dashed, and life has been wasted. Everything hinges on the fact that three things are combined in this hurdle: (1) the problem is a very subtle matter, (2) the risk of error is serious, and (3) the danger is enormous.

1. As for the subtle nature of the problem, the channels through which deeds are infiltrated by ostentation and vain conceit are extremely subtle and concealed. Hardly anyone is alert to that process, except those who are adept in the sphere of religion, keenly perceptive, wakeful at heart, and prudently cautious. How can it be detected by the stupid ignoramus and the heedless addict of sleep?

In Nishāpūr, I heard the following account from one of our scholars (may God bestow His mercy upon them): "'Aṭā' as-Sulamī (may God bestow His mercy and His good pleasure upon him) wove a garment, tailored it to perfection and made it very beautiful. Then he took it to the market and put it on display, but the draper offered a cheap price, saying: 'It has so many flaws. Look here, and here....' 'Aṭā' took it back and sat weeping bitterly. The man felt sorry, became apologetic and offered him the price he wanted, so 'Aṭā' said to him: 'The problem is not as you suppose. I work at this craft [of weaving], and I tried hard to perfect this garment, to improve it and make it beautiful, so that it would be flawless. Then, when it was displayed to someone able to detect its faults, he showed me flaws that I had failed to notice.'"

What does that say about these deeds of ours, when they are displayed tomorrow [at the Resurrection] to God 🕮? How many flaws and defects, of which we are heedless today, will become apparent in them then?

We are told that one of the righteous said: "One night at the time before dawn, I was in a room next to a main street, reciting the Qur'ānic Sūra entitled Ṭā-Hā. As soon as I had concluded the recitation, I fell into a doze, and I saw a figure descend from the sky, holding a copy of the Qur'ān in his hand. He spread it out in front of me, and there was the Sūra Ṭā-Hā! Ten merits were recorded under each word of the text, with the exception of one word. A blank space had been substituted for that word, and I saw nothing underneath it. I said: 'By God, I recited this word, but I see no reward for it, and I do not see it inscribed.' The figure said: 'You have told the truth. You did recite it, and we inscribed it, but then we heard a crier calling from the direction of the Heavenly Throne: "Erase it, and drop its reward," so we erased it.' I wept in my sleep, and I said: 'Why did you do that?' He replied: 'A man passed by [during your recitation], so you raised your voice to impress him, and away went the reward [for reciting that word].'"

2. As for the seriousness of the risk of error, ostentation and vain conceit are a terrible affliction, which can strike in the twinkling of an eye, and may ruin your worship of seventy years.

It is related that a man once entertained Sufyān at-Thawrī (may God bestow His mercy upon him) and his companions, so he said to his family: "Fetch the platter—not the one I brought on the first Pilgrimage, but the one I brought on the second Pilgrimage." Sufyān looked at him and said: "Poor wretch! He has spoiled his Pilgrimage by saying this!"

This is another aspect of the risk of error: To the slightest obedience that is immune to ostentation and vain conceit, God ﷻ assigns a value that has no end. On the other hand, the greatest amount of obedience remains without value, if this affliction strikes it, unless God ﷻ sets it right. It is reported that ʿAlī ؓ once said: "An accepted deed is absolutely not of little value. How can an accepted deed be of little value?" Someone asked an-Nakhaʿī about the reward for a certain kind of good work. He replied: "If it is accepted, its reward is incalculable."

According to Wahb: "Among those before your time, there was a man who worshipped God ﷻ for seventy years, fasting without breaking fast from Saturday to Saturday. Then he asked God ﷻ to satisfy a need, but it was not satisfied, so he reproached his lower self, saying: 'I have been ruined by you. Had there been any goodness to your credit, your need would have been fulfilled.' God ﷻ then sent down an angel, who said: 'O son of Adam! The moment when you rebuked your lower self is worth more than your previous worship [of seventy years]!'"

The intelligent person should reflect on this saying. It is surely a sign of the risk of error, that one person labours and toils for seventy years, while another takes thought for a single moment, and a moment's thought is worth more in God's sight than the worship of seventy years! Yet you lose that opportunity unnecessarily! By God, that is the greatest risk of error! To neglect it is surely the most serious loss. If a mode of conduct is so worthless and so fraught with danger, you must guard against it and avoid it.

Because of this kind of consideration, those worshipful servants who are endowed with faculties of discernment have investigated these kinds of subtleties. They have concerned themselves with these kinds of secrets, in order to become familiar with them, first of all, then to monitor them and take precautions against them, in second place. They have not been satisfied with the multiplicity of good deeds in the realm of external appearance, and they have said: "It is a matter of pure intent, not of multiplicity." They have also said: "A single jewel is better than a pearl."

As for those who have little knowledge, and whose interest in this topic is slight, they are ignorant of the deeper meanings, and heedless of the faults within their hearts. They are preoccupied with compelling their lower selves to bow and make prostration [in the ritual prayer], to abstain from food and drink, and so on. They are deluded by the number and frequency [of their acts of worship], and do not consider the spiritual benefits and purity of heart involved. The number of walnuts is not sufficient, if they contain no kernels. The erection of roofs is useless, if their underlying structures are not firmly established. No one understands these realities, except those who manifest true knowledge of God ﷻ. He is the Custodian of right guidance, by His gracious favour.

3. As for the enormity of the danger, there are several aspects to consider: First, the One who is Worthy of worship is a Sovereign of endless Majesty and Might, and you are indebted to Him for countless and innumerable blessings. You have a body that is flawed by hidden faults, afflicted by many afflictions, and your situation is perilous, since your lower self is rushing towards a mishap that may befall you. The servant therefore needs to produce work that is pure and sound, from a body that is flawed and a lower self that is always inclined to wickedness, always instigating evil. He must produce that work in a manner befitting the Lord of All the Worlds, in keeping with His Majesty, His Might, and the abundance of His blessings and His gracious favour. Your work must be worthy of His approval and acceptance, otherwise you will forfeit the

enormous profit, which the lower self cannot bear to lose, and you may even be afflicted by a disaster that you simply cannot endure. This, by God, is a dreadful and terrible prospect.

As for the Majesty and Might of the Sovereign, the righteous angels-brought-near are active in His service through the watches of the night and the day. Some of them have been in an upright posture [*qiyām*] since God ﷻ created them. Some have been in a bowing posture [*rukūʿ*] and some in prostration [*sujūd*], while some have been engaged in glorification [*tasbīḥ*] and *tahlīl* [proclaiming: "There is no god but God (*lā ilāha illa 'llāh*)"]. The one who is standing upright does not conclude his standing, nor the one who is bowing his bowing, nor the one in prostration his prostration, nor the glorifier his glorification, nor the *muhallil* [proclaimer of God's Uniqueness] his *tahlīl*, extending the sound of it till the blowing of the trumpets. Then, when they have finished this tremendous service, they all cry out together: "Glory be to You! We have not served You as You truly deserve!"

The Chief of the Messengers, the best of all creatures, the most knowledgeable and most excellent of all human beings, Muḥammad ﷺ, says [to his Lord]: "I do not count any praise as worthy of You. You are as You have praised Yourself." He is saying, in effect: "I cannot praise You with any praise that You deserve, let alone worship You as You deserve!" It is also he who said: "No one will enter the Garden of Paradise on account of his work." They said: "Not even you, O Messenger of God?" He replied: "Not even I, unless God covers me with His mercy!"

As for the abundance of His gracious favours and blessings, it is as He has said: *And if you try to reckon the bounty of God, you will never count it* (14:34). According to traditional report, He will gather people [at the Resurrection] on the basis of three lists: the list of good deeds, the list of bad deeds, and the list of gracious favours. The good deeds will be collated with the gracious favours, so that no good deed is noted without a gracious favour being noted, until the gracious favours cover and overflow the good deeds. The bad deeds and sins will remain, so what is to be done about them depends on God's will.

As for the faults and vices of the lower self, we have discussed them in their own chapter. The danger to be feared is that the servant may toil in worshipful service and persist for seventy years, heedless of his faults and his vices, so that not one of his acts of worship is accepted. He may labour for years, only to have his work corrupted by a single moment. Even worse than all that is the danger that God ﷻ may look at the servant while he is making a display of his worship and his service, seeking to impress his fellow human beings. In other words, he has presented his external appearance to God ﷻ, and his inner being to creatures, so God ﷻ will drive him into an exile from which there is no return. The only refuge is with God ﷻ!

I have heard from one of the scholars that al-Ḥasan al-Baṣrī (may God bestow His mercy upon him) was seen in a dream after his death, so he was asked about his condition, and he said: "God made me stand in His presence, and He said: 'O Ḥasan, do you remember the day when you were praying in the mosque, and people kept staring at you, so you improved the performance of your prayer? If the first part of your prayer had not been sincerely devoted to Me, I would have banished you today from My door. I would have cut you off from Me once and for all.'"

Since the matter as a whole is extremely precarious and difficult, those endowed with perceptive faculties have examined it meticulously, fearing for themselves. Some of them have gone so far as to disregard everything that makes people notice their deeds. It is related that Rābiʿa [bint Ismāʿīl al-ʿAdawiyya (may God bestow His mercy upon her)] once said: "Whatever is noticeable to me among my deeds, I count it as nothing." Someone else said: "Conceal your good deeds, just as you conceal your bad deeds." Another says: "If it is possible for you to keep a good deed in hiding, you must do so." It is also related that Rābiʿa was asked: "By what means do you hope to achieve what you hope for the most?" She said: "By despairing of the bulk of my work!"

We are told that Muḥammad ibn Wāsiʿ and Mālik ibn Dīnār once met together, and Mālik said: "Either obedience to God, or the Fire of Hell!" Muḥammad ibn Wāsiʿ said: "Either God's mercy, or the Fire of Hell!" Mālik then said: "How great is my need for a teacher like you!"

According to Abū Yazīd al-Bisṭāmī (may God bestow His mercy upon him): "I laboured at worshipful service for thirty years, then I noticed someone saying to me: 'O Abū Yazīd, His treasuries are filled with worshipful service, so, if you wish to attain to Him, you must practise humble submissiveness and feel in need of Him.'"

I heard Professor Abu'l-Ḥasan relate that Professor Abu'l-Faḍl (may God bestow His mercy upon them both) used to say: "I know that the acts of obedience I perform are not accepted in the sight of God ﷻ." He was questioned about that, so he replied: "I know what is necessary for work to be accepted, and I know that I do not meet that requirement, so I know that my deeds are not accepted." He was asked: "So why do you do them?" He replied: "Perhaps God ﷻ will improve me one day, so my lower self will become accustomed to good work. I do not need to make it accustomed to that from the outset."

Such is the state of these luminaries, and of those who are dedicated to striving and making spiritual progress, so you must be as the poet said:

> Seek friendship for yourself with 'someone' other than people,
> so that despair befalls and hopes [of them] are dashed.
> You will never catch up, at a sluggish pace, with leaders
> who have wearied themselves and succeeded in making progress.

At this point, I have decided to quote a traditional report from the truthful and trustworthy [Prophet Muḥammad] ﷺ, though we have already quoted it in more than one book. It reads as follows:

It is related on the authority of Ibn al-Mubārak (may God bestow His mercy upon him), that a man called Khālid ibn Maʿdān said to Muʿādh: "Tell me a narration [*ḥadīth*] that you heard from God's Messenger ﷺ, one that you have learned by heart and remembered every day because of its forcefulness and its subtlety." Muʿādh agreed, then he spent a long time weeping, then he said: "How I yearn for God's Messenger ﷺ and the meeting with him!" Then he said: "While I was with God's Messenger ﷺ, he mounted a riding beast and mounted me behind him. Then we traveled, and he raised his eyes towards the sky, then he said: 'Praise be to God, who decrees for His creatures whatever He wills, O Muʿādh!'

"I said: 'Doubly at your service [*labbayk*], O Chief of the Messengers!'" He said: 'I shall tell you a story that will benefit you if you learn it by heart. If you waste it, however, the evidence in your favour will be dismissed [on the Day of Resurrection] in the presence of God ﷻ. O Muʿādh, God ﷻ created seven domains before He created the heavens and the earth. To each heaven He assigned an angel as a gate-keeper and treasurer. At each of the gates of the heavens He appointed an angel as a keeper, in accordance with the status of the gate and its majesty. The guardian angels ascend with the servant's work, which has a light and radiant beams like the sun, until, when it reaches the heaven of this world, the guardians augment his work and increase it. Then, when it reaches the gate, the angel [in charge of that heaven] says to the guardians: "Take this work and use it to strike its owner in the face! I am the overseer of backbiting. If someone is guilty of backbiting people, my Lord has commanded me not to allow his work to pass beyond me to another [gate-keeper]."

'The guardian angels then ascend, the next day, bearing a righteous work that has a shining light. The guardians augment it and increase it, until, when they finally bring it to the second heaven, the angel in charge says: "Stop! Take this work and use it to strike its owner in the face! He performed it for the sake of worldly gain. My Lord has commanded me not to allow his work to pass beyond me to another [gate-keeper]." The angels then curse him [the servant] until the evening arrives.

'The guardian angels then ascend with the work of the servant who takes great delight therein. It includes charitable giving, fasting, and much piety, so the guardians augment it and increase it. Then, when they finally bring it to the third heaven, the angel on duty at the gate says: "Stop! Take this work and use it to strike its owner in the face! I am the angel in charge of arrogant pride [kibr]. My Lord has commanded me not to allow his work to pass beyond me to another [gate-keeper], for he used to treat people with arrogant pride at their meetings."

'The guardian angels then ascend with another servant's work, while it shines with the radiance of the stars and the brilliant planet. It includes a gentle murmur, a glorification [of the Lord], a fast, a ritual prayer, a Pilgrimage and a Visitation ['Umra]. Then, when they finally bring it to the fourth heaven, the angel assigned to it says: "Stop! Take this work and use it to strike its owner in the face! I am the angel in charge of vain conceit. My Lord has commanded me not to allow his work to pass beyond me to another [gate-keeper], for, when he performed an act of work, he used to infect it with vain conceit."

'The guardian angels then ascend with another servant's work, which is paraded as a bride is carried in procession to her bridegroom. Then, when they finally reach the fifth heaven, bearing that good work consisting of sacred combat [jihād], a Pilgrimage and a Visitation ['Umra], and shining like the sun, the angel on duty says: "I am the angel in charge of envy. He used to envy people for what God ﷻ had given them from His gracious favour. He was displeased with that which pleased God ﷻ. My Lord has commanded me not to allow his work to pass beyond me to another [gate-keeper]."

'The guardian angels then ascend with another servant's work, consisting of a perfect ablution, much prayer, fasting, a Pilgrimage and a Visitation ['*Umra*], Then, when they finally pass on with it to the sixth heaven, the angel on duty at the gate says: "I am the angel in charge of mercy. Take this work and use it to strike its owner in the face! He never treated any human being with mercy, and if a servant was afflicted, he would gloat over his misfortune. My Lord has commanded me not to allow his work to pass beyond me to another [gate-keeper]."

'The guardian angels then ascend with another servant's work, consisting of much charitable expenditure, fasting, ritual prayer, sacred combat, and pious caution. It has a sound like the sound of thunder, and a light like the flash of lightning. Then, when they finally bring it to the seventh heaven, the angel assigned to that heaven says: "I am the overseer of reputation, meaning celebrity and fame among the people. The owner of this work performed it with the intention of being talked about at public meetings, being highly esteemed by his fellows, and acquiring prestige in the sight of the elders. My Lord has commanded me not to allow his work to pass beyond me to another [gate-keeper]. If any work is not devoted sincerely to God 羅, it is an act of ostentation, and God 羅 does not accept the ostentatious hypocrite."

'The guardian angels then ascend with another servant's work, consisting of ritual prayer, alms-giving, fasting, Pilgrimage, Visitation ['*Umra*], good ethics and morality, taciturnity, and remembrance of God 羅. The angels of the seven heavens collaborate in removing all the obstacles to God 羅, so they stand in the presence of the Lord (Magnificent is His Majesty) and bear witness to Him that the servant's work is righteous, devoted sincerely to God 羅.

'God 羅 then says: "You are the guardians of My servant's work, and I am the Observer of what his inner being contains. He did not intend this work for My sake. He intended it for someone other than Me, and he did not devote it sincerely to Me. I know best what he intended by his work. My curse be upon him! He has deceived his fellow human beings, and he has deceived you, but he has not deceived Me, for I am the Knower of things unseen, the Overseer of what the hearts contain. No secret is hidden from Me, and nothing absent is absent from Me. My knowledge of what has been is like My knowledge of what will be. My knowledge of what has passed is like My knowledge of what remains. My knowledge of the first is like My knowledge of the last. I know the secret and what is more deeply hidden still, so how can My servant deceive Me with his work? He only deceives those creatures who do not work, and I am the Knower of things unseen. My curse be upon him!"

'The seven angels and the three thousand collaborators then say: "O our Lord, upon him be Your curse and our curse!" The people of the heavens say: "Upon him be God's curse and the curse of all those who curse!"'

Muʿādh (may God bestow His mercy upon him) wept at this point, sobbed bitterly, and said: "O Messenger of God, how can I obtain salvation from what you have described?" He replied: "O Muʿādh, you must follow your Prophet in certitude." Muʿādh said: "You are God's Messenger, and I am Muʿādh ibn Jabal. Can I somehow obtain salvation and deliverance?" He said: "Yes, O Muʿādh. If your work contains a shortcoming, you must restrain your tongue from insulting people, especially your brethren who know the Qur'ān by heart. Your knowledge of your own fault must dissuade you from insulting other people. You must not flatter yourself by blaming your brethren, nor exalt yourself by putting your brethren down. You must not put your work on display, to make yourself known among people. You must not become so involved in this world that it makes you forget the business of the Hereafter. You must not whisper to a man while another is in your presence. You must not treat people haughtily, for if you do, you will be deprived of the benefits of this world and the Hereafter. You must not speak or act obscenely at your meeting, so that people shun you because of your bad morality. You must not taunt people, and you must not rip them apart with your tongue, for if you do, the hounds of Hell will rip you apart." [This is referred to in His saying: *By the rippers ripping….* (79:2). In other words, they are tearing the flesh from the bones.]

Muʿādh said: "O Messenger of God, who is capable of these virtues?" He replied: "O Muʿādh, what I have described to you is easy for someone, if God 🌸 makes it easy for him. All that you need is to like for other people what you like for yourself, and to dislike for them what you dislike for yourself, for then you will have been saved and delivered."

According to Khālid ibn Maʿdān: "Muʿādh did not recite the Qur'ān as often as he recited this Prophetic tradition [*ḥadīth*] and mentioned it at his public meeting."

All of you have now heard this glorious Prophetic tradition, the impact of which is so great that hearts are disturbed by it, minds are bewildered by it, breasts are too narrow to bear it, and lower selves are alarmed by it. You must therefore take refuge with your Master, the God of all the Worlds, and cling to His door with humble submission, entreaty and weeping, through the watches of the night and the ends of the day, in the company of those who are humbly submissive and imploring.

There is no escape from this situation except through His mercy, and no safety from this ocean except through His favour, His enabling grace and His providential care. You must therefore wake up from the slumber of the heedless, give the matter its rightful due, and struggle with your lower self on this perilous hurdle, so that you may not perish with those who perish. God is the One whose help is sought in every case, for He is an Excellent Helper, and He is the Most Merciful of the merciful. There is no might nor any power except with God, the All-High, the Almighty.

§ SUMMARY POINTS ON IMPAIRMENTS

The gist of the matter is this: If you pay careful attention, you will see the value of obedience to God ﷻ. You will see the inadequacy of creatures, their weakness and their ignorance, so you must attach no importance to them with your heart. You must be indifferent to their praise, their commendation and their high esteem, in which there is no benefit. You must not seek any of that in exchange for your worshipful obedience. Since you notice the mean and trivial nature of this world, and the speed at which it passes away, you must also not seek it from God in exchange for your obedience.

You must say: "O lower self, the praise of the Lord of All the Worlds, and His appreciation, is better than the praise of incompetent and ignorant creatures, who do not recognise the true value of your work, and what you have endured in its performance. Far from acknowledging what you really deserve for your work and your endurance, they may well think more highly of someone who is inferior to you by a thousand degrees. They may desert you and forget you at the times of greatest need. Even if they do not do that, what do they have at their disposal, and of what are they capable? Besides, they are in the grip of God ﷻ, who handles them as He wills, and uses them for whatever purpose He wills. You must therefore be intelligent, O lower self, so that you do not waste your honourable obedience on them, and do not forfeit the praise of Him whose praise is every glory, and the gift of Him whose gift is every treasure." The poet spoke the truth when he said:

Insomnia of the eyes for other than Your sake is futile,
and their weeping for other than Your loss is wasteful.

You must also say:

O lower self, which is better, the Garden of eternity or a glimpse of this world's unlawful bounty and its wretched, fleeting rubbish? You are capable of obtaining that permanent blessing in exchange for your worshipful obedience, so do not be mean in your aspiration, vile in your intention, and base in your deeds. Look at the doves when they fly aloft, and see how their worth ascends and their value increases! You must therefore raise all your aspiration heavenwards. You must devote your heart entirely to God ﷻ, the One in whose Hand the whole matter is held. You must not waste what you have gained by your worshipful obedience. If you contemplate with care, you will see in this obedience the enormous benefits and favours bestowed upon you by God ﷻ.

First of all, He made it possible for you and gave you the means [to practise obedience]. Secondly, He removed the impediments from you, leaving you free to practise this obedience. Thirdly, He singled you out for enabling grace and assistance, and made obedience easy for you and beautified it in your heart, so that you put it into practise. Fourthly, regardless of His Majesty and His Might, His independence of you and of your obedience, and the abundance of His gracious favour unto you, He prepared for you, in exchange for this easy work, the bountiful praise and the vast reward that you do not deserve. Fifthly, He showed you grateful appreciation for that, praised you with bountiful praise for this easy work, and loved you for doing it.

All of this is due to His stupendous favour, nothing else. Were it not so, what entitlement would you have, and what would be the value of your mean and faulty work? You must therefore remember, O lower self, the gracious favour of your Lord, the All-Generous, the All-Compassionate ﷻ, in granting you the blessing of this worshipful service. You must be ashamed of attaching importance to the work, and attribute the grace and favour to God ﷻ in every case. Your sole preoccupation, after achieving this worshipful obedience, must be humble entreaty and supplication to God ﷻ, imploring Him to accept your obedience. You have surely heard the saying of His Bosom Friend [*Khalīl*], Abraham ﷺ, when he had concluded his service in building His house [the Ka'ba], and how he implored God to bless him with acceptance. He said: *"Our Lord, accept from us! You are the All-Hearing, the All-Knowing"* (2:127). Then, when he had finished his supplication, he said: *"Our Lord, and accept the prayer of supplication!* (14:40).

If he now favours you with acceptance of this paltry merchandise, He has perfected the blessing and magnified the gracious favour, conferring so much happiness, power, glory and exaltation. He has adorned you with so many robes of honour, bounties, treasures and tokens of esteem. If the opposite is the case, however, you will suffer so much loss, forfeiture and deprivation. You must therefore attend to this matter with care, and make it your sole preoccupation.

If you are diligent in this, repeat it to your heart in the wake of your act of obedience, and seek help from God ﷻ, He will divert you from paying attention to creatures and the lower self. He will distract you from ostentation and vain conceit, and direct you towards utterly sincere devotion to God ﷻ in acts of obedience and constant remembrance of God's gracious favour, in all situations. You will achieve the best acts of obedience you could hope for, pure and containing no fault, sincere good deeds containing no blemish, and accepted acts of worship containing no deficiency.

Even if you achieve the like of this only once in your lifetime, it really amounts to very much indeed. By my life, even if it is little in number, its significance is great, its value is tremendous, its benefits are many, and its consequence is excellent. Enablement to succeed in the like thereof is glorious, and great is the servant's debt to God ﷻ for the benefit conferred. What gift is more magnificent than a gift that is accepted by the Lord of All the Worlds? What merchandise is more splendid than merchandise that is chosen and approved by the Lord of All the Worlds?

You must therefore pay close attention, O miserable wretch, and beware of being among the deprived. If the matter proceeds in accordance with all of this advice, you will be among those who are sincerely devoted to God ﷻ, afraid of offending Him, mindful of His gracious favours, and well pleasing [to Him]. You will have left this perilous hurdle behind you and been saved from its disasters. You will have gained its benefits and its fruits, acquiring its noble gifts and its bountiful blessings for all eternity.

God ﷻ is the Custodian of enablement and protection, by His gracious favour and His noble generosity. There is no might nor any power except with God, the All-High, the Almighty.

THE HURDLE OF GRATITUDE

THIS IS THE hurdle of praise [*ḥamd*] and thankfulness [*shukr*]. Your next duty—may God assist you, and us, with His enabling grace!—after surmounting these hurdles, and achieving the goal of this worshipful service safe from disasters, is to give praise and thanks to God ﷻ for this enormous blessing and generous favour. That is incumbent upon you for two simple reasons: (1) to ensure that the enormous blessing will last, and (2) in order to obtain still more.

1. As for the permanence of the blessing, thankfulness is the means of securing blessings. With it they continue and persist, and without it they disappear and pass away. God ﷻ has said: God *does not change what is in a people, until they change what is in themselves* (13:11).He has also said (More Glorious is He than any other sayer): *But it was ungrateful for God's blessings, so God made it experience the garb of starvation and fear because of what they used to do* (16:112). And He has said: *What concern has God for your punishment, if you are thankful and truly believe?* (4:147). The Prophet ﷺ once said: "Blessings are untamed beasts, like the beasts of the wild, so tie them with thankfulness!"

2. As for obtaining more, just as thankfulness is the means of securing the blessing, it is also the cause of increase. God ﷻ has said: *If you are thankful, I will surely give you more* (14:7). And those who are guided aright, them He increases

in guidance (47:17). *And as for those who strive in Our cause, surely We shall guide them in Our ways* (29:69). If a wise master sees that his servant treats a favour with proper respect, he will grant him another, and consider him worthy of it. Otherwise, he will withhold that [extra favour] from him.

Blessings are of two kinds: (1) worldly and (2) religious. The worldly kind is of two types: (1) the blessing of benefit [*naf*] and (2) the blessing of protection [*daf*].

The blessing of benefit is conferred on you in the form of things that are in your interest and to your advantage. Advantages are of two sorts: (1) a nature that is sound in its health and well-being, and (2) carnal pleasures like food, drink, clothing, women, and similar benefits.

The blessing of protection is conferred by shielding you from causes of corruption and harm. It takes two forms: (1) It protects your physical body, by keeping you safe from its diseases, afflictions and illnesses. (2) It protects you from harmful influences, such as impediments of various kinds, or the evil intention of a human being, a jinnī, a savage beast, a pest, or some other creature.

As for religious blessings, they are of two types: (1) the blessing of enabling grace [*tawfīq*] and (2) the blessing of immunity [ʿ*iṣma*].

The blessing of enabling grace [*tawfīq*] means that God enables you, first of all, to accept Islam, then to follow the Sunna [exemplary custom of the Prophet 🙏], then to practise worshipful obedience.

The blessing of immunity [ʿ*iṣma*] means that He makes you immune, first of all, to unbelief [*kufr*] and polytheism [*shirk*], then to other sinful acts of disobedience. The detailed account of that can be reckoned by none but the All-Knowing Master, who has bestowed His blessing upon you. As He has said: *And if you try to reckon God's blessing, you will never count it* (14:34).

As for the permanence of all these blessings, after He has bestowed them upon you, and what is added to every part of them, that is beyond the calculating power of your imagination. They all depend on one thing, and that is thankfulness and praise for God. When a virtue has such value, and contains all this benefit, it deserves to be adhered to without the slightest neglect, for it is a precious jewel and a marvellous alchemy [*kīmiyāʾ*]. God is the Custodian of enabling grace.

You may ask: "What is the real meaning of praise and thankfulness? What is their spiritual significance and their legal status?"

You should therefore know that the scholars have drawn a distinction between praise and thankfulness. According to their interpretation, praise [*ḥamd*] is one of the forms of glorification [*tasbīḥ*] and *tahlīl* [proclaiming: "There is no god but God (*lā ilāha illa 'llāh*)"], so it is one of the external acts of worship. Thankfulness, on the other hand, is one of the forms of patience and delegation [*tafwīḍ*], so it is one of the internal acts of worship. Thankfulness is contrary to ingratitude, while praise is contrary to blame. Praise is more common and more frequent, while thankfulness is less frequent and more special. God ﷻ has said: *And few of My servants are very thankful* (34:13).

It is thus established that praise and thankfulness are two distinct concepts. Furthermore, praise means commending someone for good behaviour. This point is stressed by our own Shaikh (may God bestow His mercy upon him).

As for thankfulness, the experts have had much to say about its meaning. According to Ibn ʿAbbās ﷺ: "Thankfulness is worshipful obedience, with all the limbs and organs, to the Lord of all creatures, in secret and in public." One of our own shaikhs held a similar view, for he said: "Thankfulness is the performance of acts of worshipful obedience, both outwardly and inwardly." He then reconsidered and said: "It is the avoidance of sinful acts of disobedience, both outwardly and inwardly."

Another said: "Thankfulness is guarding against the voluntary commission of sinful acts of disobedience against God. You must stand guard over your heart, your tongue and your limbs, so that you do not disobey God ﷻ with any of these three, in any way at all." The difference between his opinion and that of the first Shaikh is that he [this second Shaikh] ﷺ has assigned a definite significance to being on guard, in addition to avoiding sinful acts of disobedience. As for avoidance of the sinful act of disobedience, it is simply a matter of not committing that act in the presence of its stimulants. It is not in itself an acquired virtue, with which the servant is preoccupied and immunized against ingratitude.

According to our own Shaikh ﷺ: "Thankfulness means extolling the Benefactor for His benefaction, in a manner that precludes disrespect for the Benefactor and ingratitude towards Him."

You may say: "If thankfulness means extolling someone who does good work, in recognition of that good work of his, it is surely correct to maintain that thankfulness flows from God to the servant."

That is a good point, and we have discussed its detailed implications in the book entitled: *Revival of the Religious Sciences* [*Iḥyā' 'Ulūm ad-Dīn*], as well as in other books. The crux of the matter, however, is that thankfulness from the servant is a reverence that precludes disrespect for One who treats him well, and it signifies remembering the Benefactor's benefaction, the virtue of the thankful in his thankfulness, and the vice of the ingrate in his ingratitude.

The least that is due to the Benefactor for His benefaction is that it should not be used as an instrument of disobedience. How vile is the condition of someone who uses the Benefactor's benefaction as a weapon with which to disobey Him! It is therefore incumbent on the servant, if he is to fulfil the duty of thankfulness in its true sense, to have a reverence for God ﷻ that forms a barrier between him and his sinful acts of disobedience, based on the remembrance of His blessings. If he meets this fundamental requirement, then matches it with serious effort in obedience and dedicated commitment to the performance of service, the benefaction has been treated with all due respect, for guarding against sinful disobedience is absolutely essential. God is the Source of enabling grace!

You may ask: "In what context is thankfulness appropriate?"

You should therefore know that it is appropriate in the context of both worldly and religious blessings, in accordance with their respective values. As for hardships and misfortunes is this world, affecting yourself, your family or your property, the scholars have discussed the question: "Is thankfulness for them incumbent on the servant?" Some of them have said: "Thankfulness for them, as such, is not incumbent on the servant. The only necessary response to them is patient endurance. As for thankfulness, it is for blessings, not for anything else." They have also said: "There is no hardship that is not accompanied by God's blessings, so thankfulness is required for the blessings associated with the hardship, but not for the hardship itself."

Ibn 'Umar ؓ was referring to those blessings [associated with hardship] when he said: "I have never been afflicted with an affliction, unless it contained four blessings bestowed on me by God ﷻ: (1) It did not affect my religion. (2)

It was not greater than the blessings. (3) I was not deprived of contentment with it. (4) I hoped for the reward for suffering it."

It has also been said: "Those blessings include the fact that hardship is transitory, not permanent, and that it comes from God 🕮, not from anyone other than Him. If it is caused indirectly by a creature, it is to your credit against him, not to his credit against you. The servant is therefore obliged to be thankful for blessings associated with hardship."

Others have said, expressing the preferred opinion of our own Shaikh (may God bestow His mercy upon him): "The hardships of this world are among those things for which the servant must be thankful, because those hardships are blessings in reality, since they expose the servant to enormous benefits, abundant rewards and generous compensations in the Hereafter. The pain of these hardships seems like nothing beside them, and what blessing is greater than this?

"For the sake of comparison, consider the situation where someone makes you drink a nasty, bitter medicine to remedy an ailment, or subjects you to phlebotomy or blood-cupping to cure a serious and dangerous disease. That treatment restores you to psychological health, physical well-being and a comfortable way of life, in spite of the pain it makes you suffer from the bitterness of the medicine, or the wound inflicted in the blood-letting operation. In reality, it is a tremendous blessing and an obvious favour, even if its outer form is so disgusting that human nature recoils from it, and the lower self is repelled by it. You will not only praise the physician who provided you with this treatment, but do all you possibly can for his benefit."

As you are surely aware, the Prophet 🕮 praised God and thanked Him for adversities, just as he thanked Him for occasions of delight, when he said: "Praise be to God for what causes grief and what causes happiness!" You must also recall His saying (Magnificent is His Majesty): *It may happen that you hate a thing in which God has placed much good* (4:19). What God calls good is more than your imagination can conceive!

This view is corroborated by the fact that blessings are not good because of pleasure and what the lower self desires by its instinctive nature. A blessing [*ni'ma*] is that which causes increase in the exaltation of spiritual degrees. That is why it is called *ni'ma*, in the sense of increase [*ziyāda*]. If hardships become a cause of increase in the servant's nobility and the exaltation of his spiritual degree, they are blessings in reality, even if they are counted as adversities and trials because of their external appearance. You must understand that successfully!

You may ask: "Is the thankful servant more virtuous, or the one who is patiently enduring?" You must therefore know that someone said: "The thankful servant is more virtuous, on the strength of God's saying: *And few of My servants are very thankful* (34:13)."

He has thus included them among the most special of the special few. He has also said, in praise of Noah 鷺: *He was a very thankful servant* (17:3). He has described Abrahām 鷺 as: *Thankful for His bounties* (16:121). And He has also commended him because he was at the spiritual station of benefaction and well-being.

That is why someone said: "To be blessed and to be thankful [for the blessing] is dearer to me than being afflicted and enduring [the affliction] with patience." According to someone else, however: "He who endures with patience is actually more virtuous, because his suffering is greater, so he is entitled to greater reward and higher spiritual station." God 鷺 has said [of the Prophet Job 鷺]: *We found him patient, an excellent servant indeed!* (38:44). He has also said: *Surely those who are patient will be paid their wages in full without reckoning* (39:10). And He has said: God *loves those who are patient* (3:146).

In reality, someone who is thankful [*shākir*] cannot be other than patient [*ṣābir*], and someone who is patient cannot be other than thankful. That is because, if someone is thankful in the abode of trial and tribulation, he is undoubtedly bound to experience a trial that he endures with patience. He cannot be impatient, since thankfulness means reverence for the Benefactor, to an extent that precludes disobeying Him, and impatience is a form of disobedience.

If someone is patient, he is bound to receive a blessing, for, as we have mentioned, hardships are a blessing in reality, in the primary sense. His patience is therefore thankfulness, in reality, if he is patient in enduring hardships, because he restrains himself from impatience as a mark of reverence for God 鷺. This is thankfulness itself, since it is a reverence that precludes disobedience.

Furthermore, in the case of someone who is thankful, he precludes himself from ingratitude, if he patiently refrains from disobedience, moves himself to thankfulness, and is patient in obedience. He thus becomes patient in reality. In the case of someone who is patient, he extols God 鷺 to the point where his reverence for Him precludes him from impatience with what afflicts him, and that reverence moves him to patience. He has thus given thanks to God ﷻ, and so become thankful in reality.

Moreover, restraining the lower self from ingratitude, despite its inclination thereto, is a hardship that is endured with patience by the thankful servant. As for the enabling grace and immunity bestowed upon the patient servant, they constitute a blessing for which he gives thanks, so neither of the two [patience and thankfulness] can be separated from the other. Their inseparability is also due to the fact that they are inspired by a single perception, and that is the perception of rectitude, according to some of our scholars.

For all these reasons, we maintain that neither of the two [patience and thankfulness] can be separated from the other. You must therefore understand all this correctly. God is the Source of enabling grace!

§ SUBTLETIES OF GRATITUDE

It is therefore incumbent upon you, O man, to spare no effort in surmounting this relatively easy hurdle, for the benefit is great, glorious in essence and tremendous in worth. You must also consider two fundamental points:

1. The blessing is only conferred on someone who truly understands its value, and the only one who truly understands its value is the thankful servant. The proof of our assertion is the saying of God ﷻ in the story about the ingrates and the response they received: *"Are these the ones whom God favours among us?"* Is not God Best Aware of those who are thankful? (6:53).

Those ignoramuses supposed that the mighty blessing and the generous favour would only be granted to people wealthier than the believers, and more noble in lineage and descent. They said: "Of all the slaves and the free, why should these paupers get what they claim? They have been given this mighty blessing because of their claim, instead of us!" Then they asked, in an arrogant and derisive manner: *"Are these the ones whom God favours among us?"* (6:53). God ﷻ responded to them with this brilliant remark: *Is not God Best Aware of those who are thankful?* (6:53).

He was saying by implication: "The Noble and Generous Master bestows His blessing only on those who truly understand its worth, and none truly understand its worth except those who accept it with heart and soul, prefer it to anything else, do not worry about the trouble they went through in the process of obtaining it, and then stand constantly at the door, giving thanks for the blessing.

"It was in Our sempiternal knowledge that these weaklings would truly understand the value of this blessing, and would be thankful for it. They were therefore more deserving of this blessing than you, regardless of your wealth and your riches, your prestige in this world and your entourage, your lineage and your pedigree. The only blessing that interests you is this world and its vanities, pedigree and lineage, not religion, knowledge and understanding of the truth. You revere and take pride in nothing but that. You would hardly accept this religion, knowledge and truth, except as a favour to the one who brought it to you, because you consider it so trivial and care so little about it.

"As for these weaklings, they sacrifice themselves for that, and expend their spirit for its sake. They are not worried about what they lose, or what enemies they face. You must therefore know that they are the ones who truly understand the value of this blessing, and that reverence for it is firmly rooted in their hearts. The loss of everything else is unimportant to them, and they gladly endure every hardship for its sake, so they immerse their whole lives in thankfulness for it. That is why they are entitled to this noble favour and mighty blessing, in Our sempiternal knowledge, and We have singled them out for it, instead of you."

The same applies to every group of people whom God ﷻ has singled out for one of the blessings of religion, in the form of knowledge or of practise, so you will find them to be, in reality, the people most aware of its value, those with the most intense reverence for it, those most vigorous in its acquisition, those who honour it most highly, and those who are most persistently thankful for it.

As for those whom God has deprived of that [blessing of religion], He has deprived them because of their scant concern and lack of reverence for its true worth, after the sempiternal foreordainment. If reverence for knowledge and worship, in the hearts of the common folk and the marketers, had been like the reverence in the hearts of the scholars and those devoted to worship, they would not have preferred their market and would have thought nothing of forsaking it.

Suppose a jurist [*faqīh*] succeeded in solving a difficult and complex problem. His heart would be so relieved, and he would feel so happy! That solution would occupy a such a glorious place in his heart, that even if he happened to find a thousand gold coins, their discovery would not match it. He may be so interested in a problem in the sphere of religion, that he ponders it for a year, or ten or twenty years, or even longer, without finding that too much and without becoming bored. God ﷻ may then provide him with understanding of the problem, so he will count that as a most enormous favour and a most superb blessing. He will see it as making him richer than any rich man, and nobler than any noble.

A similar problem may be explained to a common man, or to lazy student, who regards himself as equal [to the jurist] in the desire for knowledge and the love of it, but he will not listen with proper attention. If the explanation is very lengthy, he may become bored or fall asleep. Even if the solution becomes clear to him, he will not consider that to be of any great importance.

Comparable to the jurist is the penitent returning to God ﷻ. He strives so hard, and tirelessly persists in spiritual exercise, restraining the lower self from carnal desires and pleasures, and bridling the members of the body in all situations of movement and of rest. God may then enable him to complete two cycles of ritual prayer [*rakʿatain*] with due propriety and in a state of purity. For so much humble submission to God ﷻ, He may grant him an hour of intimate converse in a state of serenity and sweetness. If he achieves that once in a month, or once in a year, or even once in his whole life, he will consider it a most superb favour and a most enormous blessing. It will make him so happy, and he will be so thankful to God ﷻ. He will think nothing of the hardships he has undergone, the weariness of those nights of vigil, and the pleasures that have escaped him.

Now consider those who claim to be fond of acts of worship, keen to obtain something from them. If what they need, in order to obtain the like of this pure worship, is to go without a morsel of their supper, or to refrain from talk that does not concern them, or to make their eyes lose an hour of sleep, their lower selves will find that intolerable, and their hearts will not be pleased. Even in the rare case where they happen to experience an act of worship in a state of serenity, they do not count that as a matter of importance, and they do not accord it many thanks. The only occasions when their happiness blooms, and they express their praise prolifically, are when they obtain a silver coin, or when they receive a piece of bread with some tasty broth, or when they enjoy a long slumber in a good state of physical health. On those occasions they say: "Praise be to God! This is from God's gracious favour."

How can these heedless and incompetent types be on a par with those fortunate ones who exert themself with serious and dedicated effort? These miserable wretches have come to be deprived of all this benefit, while those enabled to obtain it are triumphantly successful. That is how the matter has been determined by the Wisest of judges, for He is the Best Aware of those who are aware. This is the import of His saying: *Is not God Best Aware of those who are thankful?* (6:53).

You must therefore understand this well, and give it the attention it deserves. You should also know that you are never deprived of something good that you desire, except because of your own lower self. You must therefore spare no effort in order to comprehend the value of God's blessing. You must revere it with the reverence it deserves, so that you may be worthy of it and of its bestowal. God will then grant you its continuance, as He has granted it to you initially, in accordance with what we have mentioned in the second fundamental point. He is indeed the Kind One, the All-Compassionate.

2. The second fundamental point is that the blessing is only removed from someone who does not truly understand its value. He who does not truly understand its value is the ingrate who is ungrateful for it, and who does not give thanks for it. The proof of that is His saying: *Recite to them the tale of him to whom We gave Our signs, but he sloughed them off, so Satan overtook him and he became one of those who are led astray. And had We so willed, We could have raised him thereby, but he clung to the earth and followed his own passion. His likeness is therefore as the likeness of the dog; if you attack him, he pants with his tongue out, and if you leave him, he pants with his tongue out. Such is the likeness of the people who deny Our signs. So narrate to them the story, for then they may reflect.* (7:175,176). God ﷻ is saying by implication:

> We blessed this servant with enormous blessings and momentous favours in the sphere of religion. We thereby enabled him to acquire the supreme rank and the lofty station at Our door, so that he could become exalted in Our sight, mighty in worth and great in prestige. But he was ignorant of the value of Our blessing, so he inclined towards this mean and despicable world, and preferred the base and vile desire of his lower self. He did not know that this world, in its

entirety, weighs less in God's sight than one of the blessings of religion, and is not equal in His sight to the wing of a gnat.

He was thus in the position of the dog, which cannot distinguish honour and comfort from disparagement and hardship, nor exaltation and nobility from wretchedness and meanness. Just like the dog, he pants with his tongue out in both situations. Generous favour, as he sees it, consists entirely of a piece of bread to eat, or the bones that are tossed to him from a table. It makes no difference whether you seat him on a couch beside you, or make him stand in the dust and dirt in front of you. As far as he is concerned, his favour and blessing amount to no more than that [bread or bones].

This is the bad servant, since he is ignorant of the value of Our blessing, and does not recognise the true worth of the generous favour We have bestowed upon him. His perceptive faculty is weak, and his behaviour in the station of nearness is bad, because of the attention he pays to others apart from Us, and his preoccupation with this vile world and trivial pleasure. We have therefore brought him under strict control, placed him in the court of justice, and subjected him to the rule of Omnipotence [*Jabarūt*]. We have stripped him of all Our robes of honour and Our noble gifts, and removed familiarity with Us from his heart. He has thus been stripped naked of all that We had bestowed upon him from Our gracious favour. He has become a banished dog and an accursed rebellious devil.

We take refuge with God, then again we take refuge with God from His displeasure and the pain of His chastisement! He is indeed Kind and Compassionate with us.

You should be content with the analogy of a king who honours a servant of his, by conferring his own fine robe upon him, drawing him close to his royal presence, placing him above his other servants and chamberlains, and commanding him to cling to his door. Then he commands the construction of palaces for that servant's use, in another place, as well as the erection of couches and tables for his sake. He also provides him with beautiful maidservants and appoints manservants to work for him. When the servant returns [to his own palace] from the king's service, his royal master seats him there as a king who is served and honoured. Between his situation of service and that of his kingship and authority, the space is no more than an hour of the day, or even less.

If this servant looks to the side of this king's door, and takes notice of a stableman who is eating a loaf of bread, or a dog that is chewing a bone, he will be distracted from the service of the king. He will fail to pay attention to the robes of honour and the gracious favour he has received, so he will rush over to that stableman, stretch out his hand and ask him for a piece of the loaf, or compete with the dog for a bone, for he will envy them both and think highly of what they have at their disposal.

If the king sees him in this condition, he will surely say: "This is a stupid, unambitious fool, who does not realise the value of our noble generosity. He does not recognise the worth of the dignity we have bestowed upon him, by clothing him with robes of honour and drawing him close to our presence, as well as granting him our caring attention and commanding that he should be given treasures and all kinds of favours. This is nothing but a dropout, an ignoramus of little discernment. Strip him of his robes of honour and drive him away from our door!"

This is the state of the scholar, if he inclines towards this world, and of the worshipful servant if he follows passionate desire, after God has honoured him with His worshipful service and intimate knowledge of His favours, His Sacred Law [*Sharīʿa*] and His judgements. Since he has failed to recognise the value of that honour, he will end up with the meanest thing in the sight of God ﷻ and the most contemptible in His sight, for he will desire it and seek it greedily. It will loom larger in his heart and be dearer to him than all those splendid blessings he has received, in the form of knowledge, worshipful service, wise insights and real experiences.

The same applies in the case of someone whom God specially favoured with various kinds of His enabling grace and His protection, whom He adorned with the lights of His service and His worship, whom He regarded with compassion in most of his moments, whom He extolled to His angels, to whom He granted leadership and dignity at His door, on whom He conferred the right of intercession, and whom He appointed to the station of the mighty. It came to the point where, if he appealed to God, He would answer him and declare Himself at his service, and if he asked Him for something, He would give to him and enrich him. If he interceded on behalf of some creatures, He would accept his intercession on their behalf, and make him well pleased. If he swore an oath by Him,

He would endorse it and fulfil it. If something occurred to his mind, He would grant it to him before he asked for it with his tongue.

Suppose this were someone's condition, but he did not truly understand the value of these blessings, or did not recognise the worth of this position, so he turned away from all that towards a wicked selfish passion, with no sense of shame, or a piece of worldly rubbish with no permanence to it. Suppose he paid no attention to those generous favours, robes of honour, presents, benefits and gifts, nor to what he had been promised and prepared for him in the Hereafter, in the form of tremendous reward and abundant and lasting bounty. How vile that person would be! What a bad servant he would be! How great would be his peril, if he did but know, and how atrocious his conduct, if he did but understand!

We beseech God, the Gentle, the Compassionate, to improve us with the splendour of His grace and the abundance of His mercy. He is indeed the Most Merciful of the merciful.

It is therefore incumbent upon you, O man, to spare no effort in order to understand the true value of the blessings you receive from God ﷻ. When He blesses you with the blessing of religion, you must beware of paying attention to this world and its vanities, for that would be nothing but a kind of disdain, on your part, for the blessings of religion entrusted to you by your Lord. You have surely heard His saying to the Chief of the Messengers: *We have given you seven of the oft-repeated [verses] and the Mighty Qur'ān. Strain not your eyes toward that which We cause some wedded pairs among them to enjoy, and be not grieved on their account, and lower your wing for the believers* (15:87,88). God ﷻ is saying by implication:

> For everyone who has been given the Mighty Qur'ān, it becomes a duty never to regard this vile world with a look of delight and approval, in addition to having no desire for it. He must be constantly thankful to God for that [gift of the Mighty Qur'ān], for it is the gracious favour eagerly sought by His Bosom Friend [*Khalīl*] Abraham ﷺ, who wished that He would confer it upon his father, but He did not do so. Then His Chosen Friend [al-Muṣṭafā] ﷺ longed for Him to confer it upon his paternal uncle, Abū Ṭālib, but He did not do so.

As for the vanities of this world, they are the rubbish that He dumps on every unbeliever, Pharaoh, apostate, atheist, ignoramus and profligate, they being the most despicable of His creatures in His sight, until they drown in those vanities. He keeps the rubbish of this world away from every Prophet, special friend, champion of the Truth, scholar and worshipful servant, they being the dearest to Him of all His creatures, so they hardly acquire a piece of bread to eat and a tattered cloak to wear. He favours them with that which does not stain them with its filth. Speaking to Moses and Aaron ﷺ, He said (More Glorious is He than any other sayer):

> If I wished to adorn you with an adornment [of this world], so that Pharaoh would know, when he saw it, that his power was incapable of producing it, I would do so, but I am withholding this world from you and making you averse to it. I do likewise with My saintly friends. I drive them away from its bounty, as the caring shepherd drives his camels away from the pools of dung. I surely keep them from enjoying its comfort and its pleasant life, and that is not because of their unimportance to Me, but in order to perfect their share of My gracious favour.

He has also said:

> *And were it not that mankind would have become one community, We might well have appointed for those who disbelieve in the All-Merciful, roofs of silver for their houses and stairs [of silver] for them to mount, and, for their houses, doors and couches [of silver] on which to recline, and ornaments of gold. Yet all that would have been but a provision of the life of this world, and the Hereafter with your Lord would have been for the truly devout.* (43:33-35)

Notice the difference between the two situations, if you are perceptive, and say: "Praise be to God, who has favoured us with the favours of His saints and His special friends, and has dispelled from us the trial of His enemies, so that we may be happy and experience the most abundant thankfulness, the greatest praise, the most copious benefit and the mightiest blessing, which is Islam." That [blessing of Islam] is the most excellent of all, so you must not abate your thankfulness for it throughout your night and your day. If you are incapable of recognizing its true worth, you should know for a fact that, even if you were created at the beginning of this world, and engaged in thankfulness for the blessing of Islam from the very first moment till eternity, you would not complete that [thankfulness]. You would leave some of the duty unfulfilled, because the gracious favour of that blessing is so tremendous.

You should also know that the space [available in this book] does not allow me to discuss the full extent of my knowledge concerning the value of this blessing. Even if I dictated a million sheets of paper on the subject, the extent of my knowledge would reach beyond that. I must confess, however, that what I know, beside what I do not know, is like a drop in all the oceans of this world. You have surely heard—woe unto you!—His saying to the Chief of the Messengers 🕊: *You did not know what the Book was, nor what the faith* (42:52). Until He said to him: *And [God] taught you what you did not know. God's grace towards you has been tremendous* (4:113). God 🕊 said to a group of people: *It is rather that God is treating you with gracious favour, inasmuch as He has guided you to faith, if you are honest* (49:17).

You have surely heard the saying of the Prophet 🕊, when he heard a man say: "Praise be to God for Islam!" He said to him: "You are praising God for a tremendous blessing!"

When the bringer of glad tidings [about Joseph] came to Jacob 🕊, he said: "In what religion did you leave him?" The man replied: "In the religion of Islam." Jacob then said: "The blessing is now complete!"

Someone said: "No statement is dearer to God 🕊, or more expressive of thankfulness in His sight, than for the servant to say: 'Praise be to God, who has blessed us and guided us to the religion of Islam!'"

Beware of neglecting thankfulness for Islam, and of being mistaken about your present condition with regard to Islam, true knowledge, enabling grace and immunity. Where that is concerned, there is no room for false security and heedlessness, for matters depend on the ultimate consequences. Sufyān ath-Thawrī (may God bestow His mercy upon him) used to say: "Whenever someone feels too secure about his religion, he will be dispossessed."

Our own Shaikh (may God bestow His mercy upon him) used to say: "When you hear about the state of the unbelievers and their everlasting sojourn in the Fire of Hell, do not feel secure about yourself, for the matter is at risk. You cannot tell what the outcome will be, nor what has been predestined for you in the decree of the Unseen, so do not be deceived by the clarity of the times, for beneath it lie the obscurities of misfortunes."

One of the shaikhs used to say: "O you who are deceived by immunities, beneath them lie all kinds of adversities. God graced Iblīs with various forms of

His immunity, though he was doomed in His sight to the realities of His curse. He also graced Bal'ām with the lights of His friendship, though he was doomed in His sight to the realities of His hostility."

'Alī ﷺ is reported as having said: "Many a one is misled by the good treatment he receives. Many a one is deceived by the good things that are said about him. Many a one is deluded by the fact that he is granted pardon." Dhu'n-Nūn was asked: "By what is the servant most likely to be deceived?" He said: "By gracious favours and generous gifts." That is why God ﷻ has said: *We shall lead them on by steps from whence they do not know* (68:44).

According to the masters of intimate knowledge [this means]: "We shall grant them abundant blessings, and make them forget to be thankful." As the poet said:

> You have thought well of the days, since they have been good,
> and you have not feared the evil of what destiny may bring.
> Your nights have been peaceful, so you have been deceived by them,
> for it is during the calm of the nights that trouble occurs.

You must also know that, whenever you come to be closer [to the Lord], your situation is more perilous and more difficult, performance of the task [of worship] is harder and more delicate, and the danger to you is greater. The higher something rises, the harder will be the fall, if it topples down. As someone said in poetic verse:

> Birds do not fly and rise aloft [indefinitely];
> as they fly up, so do they fall to earth.

There is therefore no justification whatsoever for overconfidence, neglect of thankfulness, and failure to appeal for protection. Ibrāhīm ibn Ad'ham used to say: "How can you feel secure, when Abraham ﷺ, the Bosom Friend [al-Khalīl], used to say: '*My Lord, make this territory safe, and preserve me and my sons from serving idols*' (14:35). And Joseph ﷺ, the Champion of the Truth [aṣ-Ṣiddīq] used to say: '*Let me die as one who is truly submissive [to You]*'" (12:101).

Sufyān ath-Thawrī never ceased saying: "O God, save, save!"—as if he were aboard a ship and afraid of drowning. I have heard that Muḥammad ibn Yūsuf (may God bestow His mercy upon him) once said: "I observed Sufyān ath-Thawrī one night, and he wept the whole night through, so I said to him: 'Is this weeping of yours on account of sins?' He waved a straw, and said: 'Sin is less important to God than this. All that I dread is that God may strip me of Islam and refuge with God.'"

I also heard one of those who know by experience say: "One of the prophets ﷺ asked God ﷻ about the case of Balᶜām and his banishment after those signs and noble favours, so God ﷻ explained: "He was not thankful to Me for what I gave him, not for a single day. Had he been thankful to Me for that, just once, I would not have dispossessed him.'"

You must come to your senses, O man, and observe with very great care the principle of thankfulness and praise to God for His blessings in the sphere of religion. The loftiest of those blessings are Islam and true knowledge, while the lowliest of them are, for example, the successful utterance of a glorification [*tasbīḥ*], or an immunity from talk that does not concern you. Perhaps He will complete His blessings upon you, and not test you with the bitterness of their removal. The bitterest of things, and the hardest to endure, are abasement after honour, banishment after being drawn close, and separation after communion. God ﷻ is the Noble One, the Generous, the Kind, the Compassionate.

§ SUMMARY POINTS ON GRATITUDE

The gist of the matter is this: You have taken a good close look at the tremendous favours God ﷻ has bestowed upon you, and His stupendously generous and noble gifts, which your heart cannot count and your imagination cannot encompass, and you have finally left these difficult hurdles behind you. You have found the treasures of knowledge and perceptive understanding, and been cleansed of sins and serious offences. You have overtaken the impediments, repelled the hindrances, conquered the incentives, and been saved from the impairments.

You have acquired many a noble virtue in the process, and many a lofty and dignified rank, the first of them being perspicacity and enlightenment, and the last of them being proximity and ennoblement. You have contemplated these blessings to the full extent of your intelligence and the enabling grace you have received. You have been thankful to God to the extent of your ability, so that He would keep your tongue busy with praising and extolling Him, fill your heart with His Might and His Majesty, bring you to a point where you are barred from disobeying Him, and stimulate you to serve Him, as well as you can, or to the extent of your ability, while admitting the shortfall in recognition of the true value of His gracious favour and His benefaction.

Whenever you have been negligent in thankfulness to Him, or slackened off, or made a slip, you have recovered, worked hard, turned to Him in humble submission and entreaty, and appealed to Him by saying: "O God, O my Master! As you began by blessing me with Your gracious favour, to which I had no entitlement, complete Your blessing now, again without entitlement!"

You must call out to him with the call of His saints, who have discovered the crown of His guidance, tasted the sweetness of His intimate knowledge, and feared for themselves the scorching heat of banishment and degradation, the desolation of distance and wandering astray, and the bitterness of isolation and removal. They submitted themselves humbly at the door [of His mercy], pleading for help. They stretched the palms of their hands towards Him, and cried out loud in lonely places: *Our Lord! Do not cause our hearts to stray after You have guided us aright, and bestow on us mercy from Your Presence You, only You are the Bestower* (3:8).

As I understand it—God knows best, of course!—this conveys the meaning: "We have received from You a blessing, so we are eager for another. You are the Generous Bestower, so, as You have granted us the grace of blessing at the outset, grant us the mercy of completion at the end!"

You have surely heard—woe unto you!—the first supplication [*duʿāʾ*] taught by the Lord of All the Worlds to His Muslim servants, whom He selected from among all His creatures. This supplication is expressed in His saying: *Guide us in the straight path* (1:5).

That is to say: "Set us firmly upon it and make it permanently ours." This is how you must humbly entreat Him, for the matter is tremendously important!

It has been said: "As for the wise, they have examined the misfortunes of creatures and all their trials, and they have reduced them to five: (1) Illness during absence from home; (2) Poverty in old age; (3) Death in youth; (4) Blindness after sight; and (5) Unbelief after true knowledge." Even better than that is the saying of the poet:

For everything, when you part with it, there is a substitute,
  but for God, if you part with Him, there is no substitute.

Another poet said:

> If this world lets a man keep his religion,
>   what he misses from it is not a harmful loss.

[You must entreat Him] likewise in the case of every blessing that He has bestowed upon you, and every assistance with which He has supported you in the surmounting of any of the hurdles, so that He may establish for you what He has given, and may grant you even more than you wish and desire. If you do that, you will have left this dangerous hurdle behind you, and you will have gained the two mighty and noble treasures that are right conduct and the quest for extra blessing. You will keep the existing blessings that He has granted you, so do not fear their loss, and, of the missing blessings that have not yet been granted, He will give you more than you see fit to ask for and desire, so do not fear their loss.

You will then be included among the truly knowledgeable, the scholars who act in accordance with the religion, the penitents, the pure, those who abstain from this world, those who are dedicated to service, those who conquer the devil, those who practise true devotion with the heart and the members of the body, those who curtail their expectation, those who show good will, those who are humbly submissive, those who put all their trust [in the Lord], those who delegate [their affairs to Him], those who are content, those who are patient, those who are afraid [of offending Him], those who are hopeful [of His mercy], those who are sincere, those who remember the gracious favour, and those who are thankful for the blessings of their Master, the Lord of All the Worlds.

Then, after that, you will come to be among the righteous, the ennobled, the champions of the Truth. You must therefore consider all that has been said. God ﷻ is the Custodian of enabling grace.

You may say: "If the matter is as you have described it, rare indeed is the worshipful servant of this Master, and few can ever reach this goal! Who has the strength to cope with these burdens, to meet these stringent conditions and observe these customary practises [*sunan*]?"

You must therefore know that God ﷻ says likewise: *And few of My servants are very thankful* (34:13). And: *But most human beings do not give thanks* (2:243). And: *And most of them do not understand* (5:103). And: *But most of them do not know* (6:37)

Yet that is easy for someone for whom God ﷻ makes it easy. The servant is responsible for dedicated effort, and right guidance is God's responsibility. God ﷻ has said: *And as for those who strive in Our cause, surely We shall guide them in Our ways* (29:69).

If the weak servant fulfils what is incumbent upon him, what do you think about the Lord All-Powerful, Independent, Generous and Compassionate?

You may say: "Life is short, and these hurdles are long and difficult, so how can life last until these stipulations are completely fulfilled, and these hurdles are surmounted?"

By my life, these hurdles are indeed long and the stipulations concerning them are difficult indeed. Nevertheless, if God ﷻ wishes to grant His servant special favour, He will shorten their length for him, and ease their difficulty for him, so that he will say, after surmounting them: "How close is this path [to its destination], and how short it is! What a simple matter this is, and how easy!" As I said in my own poetic verses, when I achieved this aim:

> The signpost of the highway is plain to him who seeks it,
>> but I see the hearts in blindness to the highway.
> I was amazed to see someone perish, when his salvation
>> was at hand, and I was amazed to see someone escape.

There are some who take seventy years to surmount this hurdle, some who take twenty years, some who take ten years, some who achieve it in one year, and some who surmount it in a month, or even in a week, or even in an hour. There are even some who achieve it in a split second, with special enabling grace and sempiternal providence from God ﷻ.

You surely remember the Companions of the Cave [*Aṣḥāb al-Kahf*], and how short their survival threatened to be, when they saw the change in the face of their king, Diqyānūs, so they said: *"Our Lord is the Lord of the heavens and the earth. We cry to no god beside Him, for then we would utter an enormity"* (18:14).

True knowledge came to them, and they perceived the realities contained within this path. They traversed this path, so they became delegators, trusting entirely [in God] and rightly guided. They said: *"Then seek refuge in the Cave; your Lord will spread for you of His mercy and will prepare for you a pillow in your plight"* (18:16).

All of that happened to them in the space of an hour or an instant. You surely remember the sorcerers of Pharaoh, and how barely an instant passed, when they witnessed the miracle of Moses ﷺ, before they said: *"We believe in the Lord of All the Worlds, the Lord of Moses and Aaron"* (26:47,48).

They perceived the path and traversed it, so, in a few moments or even less, they came to be among those who truly know God ﷻ, who are content with God's decree, who patiently endure His trial, who are thankful for His blessings, and who yearn for the meeting with Him. They cried: *"It is no hurt, for to our Lord we shall return"* (26:50).

We have related that Ibrāhīm ibn Ad'ham (God bestow His mercy upon him) was engaged in his worldly business, whatever that was, but then he turned away from it and set out to embark on this path. He had traveled no farther than the distance from Balkh to Marwarūdh, when he saw a man falling from the bridge into deep water, so he signalled to him: "Stop!" The man stopped at his place in the air, and so he was saved [from falling into the water and drowning]. We have also related that Rābiʿa al-Baṣriyya, as a very old slave woman, was conducted around the market of Baṣra, but nobody was interested in her because of her old age. Then one of the merchants took pity on her, purchased her for about a hundred silver coins, and emancipated her. She then chose this path and embarked on worshipful service. Barely a year had passed, before she was visited by the ascetics of Baṣra, its Qurʾān-reciters and its scholars, because of the grandeur of her spiritual station.

As for someone for whom providential care has not been foreordained, he will not be treated with gracious favour and guidance, so he must rely on his own devices. He may remain in a rift of one hurdle for seventy years, without surmounting it. He will scream and yell so very often: "How dark is this path and how difficult! How hard is this business and how perplexing!" That is because the whole matter hinges on one basic point, and that is the foreordainment of the Almighty, the All-Knowing, the Just, the Wise.

You may ask: "Why is one person singled out for special enabling grace, and another deprived of it, when both of them share the noose of servitude?"

In response to this question, a voice cries out from the awnings of Majesty: "To enjoin proper conduct, and to make known the secret of Lordship and the reality of servitude, for: *He will not be questioned as to what He does, but they will be questioned* (21:23)."

The likeness of this path in this world is the Narrow Bridge [*Ṣirāṭ*] in the Hereafter, with its hurdles, its distances and its intersections, and the differing conditions of the people traversing it. One of them passes over it like flashing lightning, one of them passes over it like the stormy wind, another like the race horse, another like the bird, while another walks on foot, another crawls so that he becomes as black as coal, another listens to the sizzling sound [of Hell], and another is seized with iron hooks and thrown into Hell.

Such is the condition of this path with its travelers in this world, for there two narrow bridges: the narrow bridge of this world and the Narrow Bridge of the Hereafter. The Narrow Bridge of the Hereafter is for the lower selves to cross, and its terrors are visible to those endowed with faculties of perception. The narrow bridge of this world is for the hearts, and its terrors are visible to those endowed with faculties of perception and intelligence. The differing conditions of those traveling in the Hereafter are due to the difference of their conditions in this world. You must consider that well and truly. God is the Source of enabling grace!

LIFE'S PATH

WHAT YOU MUST realise is that this path of ours, in both its length and its shortness, is not like the physical distances traveled by the lower selves. They traverse them on foot, so their traversing them depends on the physical strength and weakness of the lower selves. This is a spiritual path, traveled by the hearts, so you traverse it with thoughts in accordance with beliefs and perceptions. Its origin is a heavenly light and a Divine glance, which penetrates the servant's heart, so by it he sees the state of the two abodes in reality.

The servant may sometimes seek this light for a hundred years, without finding it or any trace of it. That is due to his error in the search, his shortcoming in dedicated effort, and his ignorance of the method thereof. Another may find it in fifty years, another may find it in ten, another in a day, and another in an hour or an instant, through the providential care of the Lord of Might and Glory. He is the Custodian of guidance, but the servant is commanded to strive with dedicated effort, so it is incumbent upon him to do as he has been commanded, and the commandment is predestined, foreordained. The Lord is a Just Judge, who does whatever He wills and decrees whatever He wishes.

You may say: "How great is this peril, and how difficult is this business! This weak servant is in need of so much! What is the purpose of all this work and effort, and the fulfilment of these stipulations?"

By my life, you are telling the truth when you say that the business is difficult and the peril is great. That is why He has said: *Indeed, We created the human being in trouble* (90:4). And He has said: *We offered the trust to the heavens and the earth and the hills, but they shrank from bearing it and they were afraid of it. And man assumed it. Surely he is sinful, very foolish* (33:72).

That is why the Chief of the Messengers 🙵 once said: "If you knew what I know, you would weep a great deal and laugh very little."

It is related that the crier cries from the direction of Heaven: "Would that creatures had not been created! Since they have been created, would that they knew why they have been created! Once they do know, if only they would act in accordance with what they know!" The righteous predecessors say likewise. Abū Bakr aṣ-Ṣiddīq 🙵 is reported as having said: "I dearly wish that I were green grass, so that animals would eat me, on account of my fear of the torment [in the Hereafter]." ʿUmar 🙵 is said to have heard a man recite: *Has there ever come upon the human being a while of time when he was a thing unremembered?* (76:1). He said: "If only that time would last forever!" According to Abū ʿUbaida ibn al-Jarrāḥ 🙵: "I dearly wish that I were a sheep for my family, so that my flesh would be divided, my broth would be drunk, and I would not have been created!" According to Wahb ibn Munabbih: "The human being was created stupid. Were it not for his stupidity, he would not enjoy life."

According to al-Faḍl ibn ʿIyāḍ (may God bestow His mercy upon him): "I do not envy an angel brought near [to the Lord], nor a Prophet sent as a Messenger, nor a righteous servant. Will not these be censured on the Day of Resurrection? I envy only those who have not been created."

According to ʿAṭāʾ as-Sulamī (may God bestow His mercy upon him): "If a fire was ignited, and I was told: 'If someone throws himself into it, he will become nothing,' I am afraid I would die of joy before reaching the fire!"

Well then, O man, the business is difficult, as you say. It is actually more difficult and more serious than you think and imagine, but it is a matter predestined in the knowledge of the Sempiternal, and managed by the Almighty, the All-Knowing, so the servant has no option but to spare no effort in servitude, cling to the lifeline of God, and engage in constant supplication to God ﷻ. Perhaps He will bestow His mercy upon him, so he will be saved by His gracious favour.

As for your asking about the purpose of all this, the question indicates a great heedlessness on your part. Your proper question should be: "What does all this mean in relation to what the weak servant is seeking?"

Do you know what the weak servant is seeking? The least of what he is seeking amounts to two things: (1) safety in the two abodes [this world and the Hereafter], and (2) dominion in the two abodes.

1. As for safety in the two abodes, this world, its disasters, its corruption and its calamities are such that even the angels brought near [to the Lord] are not safe from them. I have heard it related, in the story of Hārūt and Mārūt, that when the servant's spirit is transported into the sky, the angels of the heavens will say, in their astonishment: "How has this one escaped from an abode in which the best of us were corrupted?" As for the Hereafter, its terrors and its hardships are such that the prophets and messengers ﷺ will scream there: "My own self, my own self! I beg You today for my own self alone!" According to one account: "Even if a man did the work of seventy prophets, he would think that he would never be saved."

If someone wishes to be saved from the troubles of this world, let him leave them by means of Islam, for then he will be safe [*sālim*] and no affliction will befall him. If he wishes to be saved from the terrors of the Hereafter, let him enter the Garden of Paradise, for then he will be safe and no disaster will befall him. Will this be an easy matter?

2. As for dominion and noble dignity, dominion is the effective exercise of dispensation and volition. In this world, that really belongs to the saints of God ﷻ and His special friends, who are well pleased with His decree. The whole earth, both land and sea, is but one step for them. The desert and the town are gold and silver for them. The jinn and humankind, the animals and the birds are subject to them. They do not wish for anything without it becoming theirs, for they do not wish for anything except what God wills, and whatever God wills comes to be. They are not in awe of any of their fellow creatures, but all their fellow creatures are in awe of them. They serve no one except God ﷻ, and ev-

eryone but God serves them. Where do the kings of this world have one percent of this rank? They are insignificant and inferior by comparison!

As for the dominion of the Hereafter, God ﷻ says: *And when you see, there you will see a state of bliss and a grand dominion* (76:20). How splendidly the Lord of Might and Glory describes it, when He calls it "a grand dominion"!

You know that this world in its entirety amounts to very little, and that its duration from first to last is very little. The share of any one of us in this little is very little. One of us may expend his material wealth and his spirit, so that he may obtain a little amount of this little for a little while. If he does achieve that, he will be excused or even envied, and he will not begrudge the expense of his material wealth and personal effort. In the words of the poet Imru'l-Qais:

> My companion wept when he saw the road ahead of him,
>   for he was sure that we would be overtaking Caesar.
> So I told him: "Your eye must not weep! We shall either
>   gain a dominion or die, and so we shall be excused."

What can be said, therefore, about the condition of someone who seeks the grand dominion in the abode of permanent and everlasting bliss? Would he consider it too much to perform two cycles of prayer for the sake of God ﷻ, or to spend a couple of silver coins, or to stay awake for two nights? By no means! Even if he had a million selves, a million spirits and a million lives, every life greater and longer than the life of this world, he would expend all that for the sake of this mighty goal. That expense would be little indeed, and, if he finally achieved success, that would be a tremendous booty and a gracious favour from the One who gave him so much. You must therefore wake up, O miserable wretch, from the slumber of the heedless!

I also considered what God ﷻ gives the servant if he obeys Him, clings to His service, and travels this path all his life. I found that these gifts add up to forty noble awards and robes of honour, twenty in this world and twenty in the Hereafter:

1. Of the gifts bestowed in this world, the first is that God ﷻ remembers him and praises him. How great an honour for a servant, that God, the Lord of All the Worlds, should favour him with His remembrance and His praise!

2. God (Magnificent is His Majesty) thanks him and treats him with respect. If a feeble creature, like yourself, were to thank you and treat you with respect,

you would be honoured by that, so consider the honour bestowed by the God of the first and the last!

3. He loves the servant. If you were loved by the chief of a tribal encampment, or the governor of a city, you would glory in that, and benefit by it in important situations, so consider what it means to be loved by the Lord of All the Worlds!

4. He becomes a trustee for the servant, managing all his affairs.

5. He becomes for the servant a guarantor of sustenance, which He provides for him from situation to situation, without imposing any trouble or burden.

6. He becomes a defender for the servant, protecting him from every foe and shielding him from everyone with bad intent.

7. He becomes an intimate friend for the servant, who is therefore never lonely and fears no change or alteration.

8. The servant is blessed with personal esteem, so he is not degraded by the service of this world and its people. Indeed, it would not please him to be served by the kings of this world and its tyrants.

9. The servant is blessed with lofty aspiration, so he rises above being stained by the filth of this world and its people. He takes no interest in its vanities and its amusements. Like sensible men, he rises above the playgrounds of boys and women.

10. The servant acquires richness of the heart, so he becomes richer than every rich man in this world. He always feels happy and spacious in the breast. No mishap alarms him and no deprivation worries him.

11. The servant receives the light of the heart, so he is guided by that light to many kinds of knowledge, secrets and wisdom, to some of which others are not guided, except with tremendous effort and over a long span of life.

12. The servant enjoys expansiveness of the breast, so he does not feel constricted by any of this world's trials and misfortunes, nor by people's vexations and machinations.

13. The servant acquires dignity and respect in people's hearts, so the best and the worst of them revere him, and every Pharaoh and tyrant is in awe of him.

14. The servant enjoys loving affection in people's hearts. The All-Merciful instills affection for him, so you see all their hearts disposed to love him, and all their instincts moved to treat him with reverence and honour.

15. The servant derives blessing from everything in general, be it a word, a deed, an article of clothing, or a place. He derives benefit even from a speck of dust on which he treads, a place where he rests for a day, and a person who befriends him and sees him for a while.

16. The servant has the earth at his disposal, both on land and at sea, so he may travel through the air, if he wishes, or walk on the water, or cross the face of the earth in less than an hour.

17. The servant has the animals at his disposal, be they predators and savage beasts, or reptiles and the like, so the wild beasts love him and the lions wag their tails for him.

18. The servant has the keys of the earth in his possession. If he wishes for two treasures, he has only to strike with his hand, and if he needs a spring of water, he has only to stamp with his foot. Wherever he alights, a table is set before him, if he wishes to dine.

19. The servant is endowed with leadership and prestige at the door of the Lord of Might and Glory, so people depend on his service to gain access to God ﷻ, and on his prestige and his grace to obtain satisfaction of their needs from God ﷻ.

20. The servant is guaranteed a response from God ﷻ to his supplication, so he never asks God ﷻ for anything without His giving it to him, and he never intercedes on anyone's behalf without his intercession being accepted. If he swore a solemn oath by God ﷻ, He would grant him what he wished. It could even happen that, if such a servant pointed to a mountain, it would disappear, for he does not need to ask with the tongue. If something occurred to him, it would be realised, so he would not even need to gesture with his hand.

These [first twenty] are gracious gifts of honour in this world. The following are granted in the Hereafter:

21. First of all, God eases for the servant the agonies of death, of which the hearts of the prophets (blessings and peace be upon them all) were afraid, so they asked God to make them easy for them. For some, death may be like a drink

of cool water for the thirsty. God ﷻ has said: *Those whom the angels cause to die when good* (16:32).

22. Confirmation in true knowledge and faith, the prospect of losing which is the cause of all fear and alarm, of all weeping and anguish. God has said (More Glorious is He than any other sayer): *God confirms those who believe, with the Word that stands firm, in the life of this world and in the Hereafter* (14:27).

23. The delivery of spiritual comfort, fragrant perfume, good tidings, good pleasure and reassurance. As He has said: *The angels keep coming down to say: "Do not fear and do not grieve, but hear good tidings of the Garden [of Paradise] that you have been promised"* (41:30). The servant is therefore not afraid of what awaits him in the Hereafter, not does he grieve for what he has left behind in this world.

24. Everlasting life in the Gardens of Paradise and the proximity of the All-Merciful.

25. There is splendour in the secret realm for the servant's spirit, which ascends above the angels of the heavens and the earth in honour, grace and blessing. There is also splendour in the external realm for his physical body, through the celebration of its funeral procession, the thronging of the congregation at the funeral prayer held over it, and prompt attention to its preparation for burial, by which people hope to gain abundant reward, and which they count as an enormous bounty.

26. Immunity from the torment of the interrogation in the grave, and instruction in how to answer correctly. The servant is thereby kept safe from that terror.

27. The widening and illumination of the grave, so that the servant will be in one of the meadows of the Garden of Paradise until the Day of Resurrection.

28. The entertainment and honourable reception of the servant's spirit and its breath of life, for it will be installed in the abdomens of green birds, together with the righteous brethren, rejoicing and welcoming the gracious favour that God has brought them.

29. Resurrection in glory and honour, wearing fine garments and a crown, and riding a heavenly steed [*burāq*].

30. Fairness of the face and its radiant light. God ﷻ has said: *That day will faces be resplendent, looking towards their Lord* (75:22,23). And: *Some faces on that day will shine, laughing, joyous* (80:38,39).

31. Security from the terrors of the Day of Resurrection. God ﷻ has said: *Or he who comes secure on the Day of Resurrection?* (41:40).

32. Receiving the record with the right hand. Some of them will be spared the record altogether.

33. Facilitation of the reckoning. Some of them will not be subjected to any reckoning at all.

34. Weighing in the Balance. Some of them will not be weighed at all.

35. Delivery of the Basin [*Ḥawḍ*] to the Prophet ﷺ. The servant will drink a drink after which he will never be thirsty again.

36. Crossing the Narrow Bridge [*Ṣirāṭ*] and salvation from the Fire of Hell. Some of them will not even hear its sizzling sound. They will be everlastingly in what their souls desired, and the Fire will abate for them.

37. Intercession on the fields of the Resurrection, like the intercession of the prophets and the messengers.

38. The estate of eternity in the Garden of Paradise.

39. The greatest satisfaction.

40. Meeting the Lord of All the Worlds, the God of the first and the last, without qualification [*bi-lā kaif*] (Magnificent is His Majesty).

I have recounted all that to the best of my understanding and the full extent of my knowledge, with all its shortcoming and deficiency. I have nevertheless summarized and abridged the subject matter, and mentioned only the essentials and the main points. If I had treated some of that in detail, the book would not have contained it. For instance, you will notice that I have listed the estate of eternity [38 above] as one single mark of honour. If I described it in detail, it would amount to forty marks of honour, including the radiance of the houries [*ḥūr*], the palaces, the fine garments, and so on. Every item includes many details that are comprehended by none but the Knower of the unseen and the visible, the One who is their Creator and their Owner. How can we desire to know all that, when our Lord ﷻ tells us: *So no soul knows what comfort is kept secretly in store for them, as a reward for what they used to do* (32:17)?

God's Messenger ﷺ has said: "He has created in it [the Garden of Paradise] that which no eye has ever seen, of which no ear has heard, and which has never occurred to any human heart." Concerning His saying: *The sea would be used up before the words of my Lord were exhausted* (18:109)—the commentators have said:

"These are the words that God ﷻ will say to the people of the Garden, within the Garden, with gracious kindness and honour."

Such is the condition of the estate of eternity, so how can we grasp even one out of a million parts of it, when we are merely human, or how can the knowledge of a creature comprehend it? No indeed, our aspirations wane, and our minds fall short of it, and it is right and proper that it should be that way. The estate of eternity is the gift of the Almighty, the All-Knowing, in accordance with His tremendous favour and His sempiternal generosity.

However hard the workers work and the strivers strive for the sake of this momentous goal, they must know that all their effort is the least of the least beside what they need, what they seek and what they undertake. They must know that four things are indispensable to the servant: (1) knowledge, (2) work, (3) sincerity, (4) fear. First of all, he must know the path; otherwise he is blind. Second, he must put his knowledge into practise; otherwise he is blocked. Third, he must be sincere in his work; otherwise he is misled. Forth, he must not cease to be afraid and on guard against disasters, until he finds safety; otherwise he is deluded.

Dhu'n-Nūn spoke the truth when he said: "All creatures are dead, except the scholars. All the scholars are asleep, except those who put their knowledge into practise. All those who put their knowledge into practise are deluded, except those who are sincere. All those who are sincere are in tremendous danger."

Four people really make me wonder about them:

1. An intelligent person who is not a scholar. Has he no interest in knowing and understanding what lies in front of him? Why does he not investigate what he will experience after death, by studying these signs and admonitions, listening to these Qur'ānic verses [āyāt] and warnings, and checking these notions and suggestions in the lower self? God ﷻ has said: *Have they not considered the dominion of the heavens and the earth, and what things God has created?* (7:185). [And He said]: *Do they not think that they shall be raised up one awful day?* (83:4,5).

2. A scholar who does not put his knowledge into practise. Does he not consider what he knows for certain about what lies in front of him, in the form of stupendous terrors and difficult hurdles? This is the important information that you are discarding!

3. Someone who works, but is not sincere. Does he not heed the saying of God ﷻ: *So whoever hopes for the meeting with his Lord, let him do righteous work, and let him give no one any share at all in the worship due unto his Lord* (18:110)?

4. Someone who is sincere, but not afraid. Does he not notice how God (Magnificent is His Majesty) treats His special friends, His saints and His servants, who show the way between Him and His creatures? As He says to [the Prophet ﷺ] the noblest of creatures in His sight: *It has been revealed to you as to those before you: If you ascribe a partner to God your work will fail and you will be among the losers. Oh no! God you must serve, and be among the thankful* (39:65,66).

It is related that the Prophet ﷺ used to say: "[The Sūra entitled] Hūd and its sisters have turned my hair grey!"

The gist of the matter, as well as its detailed explanation, is contained in what the Lord of All the Worlds has said in four verses [*āyāt*] of the Mighty Book:

1. His saying ﷻ: *What, did you suppose that We had created you for idle sport, and that you would not be returned to Us?* (23:115).

2. His saying (Glorious is His Name): *And let every soul consider what it has forwarded for the day ahead. And practise true devotion to God. God is indeed Aware of what you do* (59:18).

3. His saying (More Glorious is He than any other sayer): *And as for those who strive in Our cause, surely We shall guide them in Our ways* (29:69).

4. He summed it all up when He said (He is the Most Truthful of sayers): *And whoever strives, strives only for himself, for God is altogether Independent of creatures* (29:6).

We seek forgiveness from God ﷻ for every slip of the foot, or transgression of the pen. We seek His forgiveness for all our sayings that do not match our deeds. We seek His forgiveness for all that we have claimed and pretended to understand about the knowledge of God's religion, despite our shortcoming therein. We seek His forgiveness for every notion that has made us guilty of affectation and pretence in a book we have written, or a speech we have composed, or a teaching we have taught. We beg Him to cause us, and you, O brethren, to put what we know into practise, with the sole intention of pleasing Him. We beg Him not to weigh that as a heavy load against us, but to set it in the scale of righteous deeds, when our deeds are returned to Him. He is indeed Munificent, All-Generous!

THE SHAIKH [IMĀM AL-GHAZĀLĪ] ﷺ CONCLUDED THIS WORK BY SAYING: "This is what we intended to mention, in explaining the nature of the journey on the path of the Hereafter, and we have been enabled to achieve the goal. Praise be to God, for by His favour good works are accomplished, and blessings descend by His grace. May God bless the best of those born into this world, who summoned his fellow human beings to the Most Excellent Master; that is to say, may He bless the Prophet Muḥammad and his family, and grant them much good and blessed peace in every situation."

NOTES

1. An allusion to the verse [*āya*] of the Qur'ān: *Surely We created the human being in the fairest stature* (95:4).

2. An allusion to the verse of the Qur'ān: *I did not create jinn and mankind except to worship Me* (51:56).

3. Qur'ān: 6:24, 8:31, 16:24, 23:83, 25:5, 27:68, 46:17, and 68:15.

4. An allusion to the verse of the Qur'ān: *Is it not He who answers the distressed, when he calls unto Him, and removes the evil, and has made you viceroys of the earth? Is there any God beside Allāh? Little do they reflect!* (27:62).

5. That is to say, it follows the prohibition included in the preceding Qur'ānic verse: *And leave trading aside* (62:9).

6. There is in reference to the verse in the Qur'ān (3:103): *And hold fast to the rope of God, all together, and do not separate. And remember God's favour upon you: how you were once enemies, then He brought your hearts together, and, by His grace, you became brothers; and how you were once on the brink of an abyss of fire, and He saved you from it. Thus does God make plain His signs to you that you may be rightly guided.*

7. This is a reference to the 94th Sūra of the Qur'ān, which includes the verses

[*āyāt*]: *Did We not expand your breast for you, and relieve you of your burden.... So truly with hardship comes ease. Truly with hardship comes ease.*

8. This is reference to the verse: *This We recite to you, [O Muḥammad], such verses and the Reminder full of wisdom* (3:58).

9. That is to say, he becomes a member of the sect called the *Murji'a* ["Postponers"], who probably acquired that name because of their great emphasis on the doctrine of *irjā'* [postponement], according to which the judgement of sinful believers must be deferred until the Resurrection.

10. The Khurramiyya sect are said to have espoused a doctrine based on *ibāḥa* [permissibility], according to which everything that is "agreeable" [khurram in Persian] is lawful.

11. That is to say, he becomes a member of the Ḥarūriyya sect, more commonly known as the Khawārij ["Seceders" or "Rebels"]. They withdrew to the village of Ḥarūrā' after they had deserted the army of ʿAlī ﷺ, in protest against his appointment of a human tribunal—instead of relying on the Word of God in the Qur'ān—to settle the violent dispute over the rightful leadership of the Islamic community.

12. This is a Sacred Tradition [Ḥadīth Qudsī], not a Qur'ānic verse. Many such Traditions are cited in this text. So subsequently, whenever God is quoted and the text is not cited as a verse of the Qur'ān or italicized as such, then it too should be taken to be a Sacred Tradition.

13. The Muʿtazila ["the Separatists"] played a major role in the development of Islamic philosophy and theology. In the long run, their methods proved too speculative and rationalistic to win favour with the majority of the scholars in the Muslim community. For a certain period, however, the doctrines of the Muʿtazila were not merely accepted by the rulers in Baghdād, but were actively imposed as the official dogma of the Islamic State.

14. The Qadariyya were so called because of their refusal to accept the doctrine of absolute Divine predestination [qadar], and their belief in the power [qudra] of human beings to create their own actions. They played a significant role in the early period of Islamic theological debate, prior to the emergence of the Muʿtazila.